DEAR MRS. KENNEDY

Also by Jay Mulvaney

Essentially Lilly

Diana and Jackie

Kennedy Weddings

Jackie: The Clothes of Camelot

JAY MULVANEY

AND PAUL DE ANGELIS

Dear Mrs. Kennedy

A WORLD SHARES ITS GRIEF

Letters, November 1963

ST. MARTIN'S GRIFFIN

NEW YORK

www.stmartins.com

See Credits and Permissions, page 232.

The Library of Congress has cataloged the hardcover edition as follows:

Dear Mrs. Kennedy : the world shares its grief: letters, November 1963 / Jay Mulvaney and Paul De Angelis.—1st ed.
    p. cm.
  ISBN 978-0-312-38615-3 (hardcover)
1. Kennedy, John F. (John Fitzgerald), 1917–1963—Death and burial. 2. Onassis, Jacqueline Kennedy, 1929–1994—Correspondence. 3. Condolence notes. I. Mulvaney, Jay. II. De Angelis, Paul.
  E842.9.D33 2010
  973.922092—dc22

                                                              2010035777

ISBN 978-1-250-04173-9 (trade paperback)

First St. Martin's Griffin Edition: November 2013

10 9 8 7 6 5 4 3 2 1

CONTENTS

INTRODUCTION

*I*n the weeks and months following the assassination of her husband, Jacqueline Kennedy received nearly one million letters. They came from every state in the nation, from every corner of the globe. The impact of President Kennedy's death, coupled with Jacqueline Kennedy's magnificent deportment throughout four terrible days in American history, was so immense that people from all walks of life wrote to a woman almost none of them knew.

These letters, which Jacqueline Kennedy pledged would be "on display at the Kennedy Library for you and your children to see," have, in fact, been tucked away in the library's archives, largely unnoticed for over forty years. Filled with emotion, patriotic sentiment, and insight, they are a poignant time capsule of one of the seminal events of the twentieth century.

Few single moments in modern history have riveted the world in the same way as JFK's killing—the 9/11 tragedy is perhaps the only other recent one. After the assassination, however, the collective grief of millions focused on a single person. From Fifth Avenue and farmhouses, from palaces and prisons, from classrooms and communes, people wrote to Jacqueline Kennedy in the fall and winter of 1963–64. For some it was a formality, a diplomatically prescribed response to the death of a world leader. For friends and relatives, it was the heart-wrenching desire to offer some small dose of consolation. But for hundreds of thousands of others, those with no connection to the Kennedys beyond a voting booth, a viewing of Jackie's televised tour of the White House, or a photograph in a newspaper, some inner force compelled them to pick up their pens and write about how the death of John F. Kennedy affected them.

Many factors gave rise to this unprecedented display of communal sympathy. To people in America, and throughout the world, John F. Kennedy represented hope for the future. His initiatives, among them his promise to land a man on the moon, captured the imagination and the spirit of the times. His famous call for service—"Ask not what your country can do for you, ask what you can do for your country"—inspired Americans of all ages, urging dedication to some larger purpose. When people looked at JFK, many saw in him their better selves.

Also, the barbaric nature of John Kennedy's death was truly shocking. It was unthinkable that the President of the United States could be shot dead in the streets of an American city. And yet it happened, in plain sight, at half past high noon.

Then, throughout the days that followed the assassination, Jacqueline Kennedy held the focus of the world. Her unwavering composure enabled Americans to start to piece together their own shattered national confidence. An insightful British journalist wrote: "She gave America the one thing it has always lacked and this is majesty."

Finally, the assassination, and its aftermath, was the first national tragedy to play out during the era of modern mass communication. For the first time in history, television news coverage continued nonstop, for four days straight, with no commercial interruption. Due to the advent of satellite technology, people across the country and around the globe were able to watch events unfold before their eyes—the eulogies and orations in the Capitol Rotunda, the killing of Lee Harvey Oswald, the walk behind the caisson to St. Matthew's Cathedral, John Kennedy Jr.'s salute to his dead father. These images were further seared into our national psyche by influential picture magazines of the day like *Life* and *Look* and later magnified by the work of pop artists like Andy Warhol. Over time they became the defining imagery of a generation.

The letters came addressed to Mrs. John F. Kennedy, The White House, 1600 Pennsylvania Avenue, Washington, D.C.; they came addressed to Madame Kennedy, Washington; to Mrs. President, America. For weeks they arrived at a rate of thirty or forty thousand letters a day. People wrote to a woman whose bravery and grace inspired them. They wrote to share their thoughts and feelings about the President whom they loved and admired and emulated. They wrote simply as an outlet for their energy. The newscaster David Brinkley expressed it this way the year after Kennedy's death: "The events of those days don't fit, you can't place them anywhere, they don't go in the intellectual luggage of our time. It was too big, too sudden, too overwhelming, and it meant too much. It has to be separate and apart." So people wrote to make sense of something that made no sense. Together, the letters form an immense chorus: a hymn of homage, longing, and grief.

"Mail was coming in and it was being piled in the corridors . . . stacked in enormous cardboard cartons, one on top of another, from the floor to the ceiling," noted Jacqueline's press secretary, Pamela Turnure, in the oral history she and social secretary Nancy Tuckerman recorded for the Kennedy Library. The deluge began on the Tuesday after the funeral, when all the letters that had been written over the weekend began to pour in from closer towns and cities. In those first days, Tuckerman recalled in 2009, neither the Pentagon nor the Justice Department was sure whether there was a wider plot. Security officials were eager for the First Lady's staff to keep up with the flow in case some letter offered clues to the mystery behind the shooting. In addition to the cards, telegrams, and letters were hundreds of packages. Once when Tuckerman entered the room where volunteers were opening up cartons containing gifts she heard a ticking sound in a box. A surge of alarm spread through the room . . . until it was discovered that the "ticker" was a mechanical toy truck from Germany meant for John Jr. that had been jostled and started up on its own. Besides toys, religious curios, flowers, and plants, came works of remarkable craftsmanship from all over the world: there were baskets and quilts of all kinds; a candle producer in Wiesbaden, Germany, sent an elaborate "Kyrie-Candle" complete with altar, robe, and crown.

After a week or two, the mail was diverted to the Old Executive Office Building next to the White House. Here offices were set up to handle the transition between administrations, and here Turnure and Tuckerman hoped to finally have enough room to sort and process the extraordinary volume of correspondence. Alas, the delivery crew got there first; Turnure wanted to "burst into tears" when she realized that the whole interior of what she had hoped would be a pristine new supply room was "stacked from the floor to the ceiling with mail."

The overwhelming majority of letters were handled by a dedicated group of friends and volunteers who opened each envelope, carefully noting the names and addresses on multiple lists. Often personally moved, they pulled aside those letters they found especially touching, but soon these files grew to the thickness of the New York telephone directory. Boxes were set up on long tables to handle specific kinds of mail like Catholic Mass cards and contributions, suggestions for memorials, requests for photos, or for the funeral Mass card designed by Jacqueline Kennedy for the President's obsequies. Correspondence from friends and leaders was supposed to be culled from the torrent of mail, marked VIP, gathered in folders, and sent to Jacqueline Kennedy in Georgetown, where she had

Volunteers reading and sorting condolence letters. Nancy Tuckerman is standing at the back of the office, leaning on the desk, with her face turned slightly toward the camera. Jacqueline Kennedy's office in the Executive Office Building, December 11, 1963. *JFK Library*

taken temporary refuge in a borrowed house. Because of the volume of mail and the tendency to use personal rather than official stationery, the importance of individual letter signers was far from obvious. Intimate friends who wrote personal messages were often even harder to recognize. "Some people would catch on right away, some didn't," noted Nancy Tuckerman in the 2009 interview. Efficiency experts from Boston brought in to consult were amazed at the undertaking but could suggest no improvements. "They thought we were doing the only thing we could do; to open them and see what they said," says Tuckerman.

Jacqueline Kennedy acknowledged the tremendous public response in a brief televised appearance on January 14, 1964. From Robert Kennedy's office at the Justice Department, seated with her two Kennedy brothers-in-law, she wore the same black suit she'd worn at the President's funeral seven weeks earlier. With a fire crackling in the background, she spoke to the American people in a low, steady voice:

> *I want to take this opportunity to express my appreciation for the hundreds of thousands of messages, nearly eight hundred thousand in all, which my children and I have received over the past few weeks. The knowledge of the affection in which my husband was held by all of you has sustained me, and the warmth of these tributes is something I shall never forget. Whenever I can bear to, I read them. All his bright light gone from the world. All of you who have written to me know how much we all loved him and that he returned that love in full measure.*
>
> *It is my greatest wish that all of these letters be acknowledged. They will be, but it will take a long time to do so. But I know you will understand. Each and every message is to be treasured, not only for my children but so that future generations will know how much our country and people in other nations thought of him.*
>
> *Your letters will be placed with his papers in the library to be erected in his memory along the Charles River in Boston, Massachusetts. I hope that in years to come many of you and your children will be able to visit the Kennedy Library. It will be, we hope, not only a memorial to President Kennedy but a living center of study of the times in which he lived and a center for young people and for scholars from all over the world. May I thank you again, on behalf of my children, and of the President's family, for the comfort your letters have brought to us all. Thank you.*

The broadcast, watched by millions around the globe, was for many the first and only time they ever heard Jacqueline Kennedy speak. Other than her famous televised tour of the White House, she had avoided interviews and speaking in public as much as possible. She was not a politician; she had no great love of public life, no need for public affection. The week after the assassination, she told journalist Theodore White, "Most people think having the world share in your grief lessens your burden. It magnifies it. . . . When this is over, I am going to crawl into the deepest retirement there is." Nevertheless, her innate sense of history, inherent courtesy, and a profound sense of gratitude to the hundreds of thousands who wrote to her impelled her to overcome her own reluctance to make a public acknowledgment.

For the group that fielded the letters, and for the former First Lady herself, the television appearance of January 14 proved a mixed blessing. For Jacqueline Kennedy, the broadcast further cemented the public's conception of her as the very model of a grieving widow, a form of psychological imprisonment from which she would eventually feel forced to escape. For the mail response team, Mrs. Kennedy's promise to acknowledge every letter not only created a formal commitment, it provoked a further avalanche of correspondence. Already the group of volunteers was struggling to keep up with the reading and organizing. Now, since it was decided that all the acknowledgment cards should be mailed out on the same day, a seemingly endless mailing list of addresses had to be collated—this in an age of typewriters and carbon paper, not computerized databases. (The zip code had been introduced only the summer before, on a purely voluntary basis. Most return addresses on condolence letters came with no postal code.)

The condolence mail response group geared up for this ever larger task. Some three thousand volunteers were brought in, and satellite locations were established at the Brookings Institute across from the White House, through congressional offices in New York City, and at Marymount College in Tarrytown, New York. Eventually every one of the letters sent in the first four months was acknowledged: on St. Patrick's Day 1964, nine hundred thousand response cards were sent out. The

*Mrs. Kennedy is deeply appreciative of
your sympathy and grateful
for your thoughtfulness*

black-bordered, cream-colored card engraved with the Kennedy family crest conveyed the poignant message. In an unprecedented move, Congress granted the President's widow franking privileges for life; thus the envelopes bore a facsimile of Jacqueline Kennedy's signature, and no stamp. In addition, Mrs. Kennedy became the first President's widow to receive Secret Service protection, as well as the first to be allocated funds for an office and secretarial staff.

Over time, Jacqueline Kennedy also responded to each of the VIP letters with a personal note. For another year or so all the mail was read, sorted, and collected, but no more acknowledgments were sent except in the case of VIP letters. By the time the official collection of condolence correspondence ended in early 1965, it totaled some 1,250,000 pieces. Many letters would find their place in the JFK Library—but they have never been put on display to the general public. Most of the items are still categorized according to the systems used by the volunteer staff who originally sorted through the torrent of incoming mail. Indeed, some boxes remain "unprocessed," and the majority of these heartfelt letters were not touched for over four decades. Yet each letter contributes something to the historical sense of the world at that time, illustrating who we were, what we felt, and how we coped with the most traumatic news in a generation.

The letters also offer a glimpse into the lost art of letter writing. In a world of text messages and e-mail, it is remarkable to experience the beauty and feel of holding and reading a handwritten letter. The graceful phrasing, the classical references, even the flowing penmanship, are heady reminders of a fast-disappearing art form. Reading through them is the equivalent of taking a master class in social grace and articulate communication.

Throughout her life Jacqueline Kennedy was famous for her handwritten notes, filled with humor, often showing a biting wit, always insightful. When she died in 1994, many also mourned the passing of an era. The world Jacqueline Kennedy represented, the world of beautiful manners, measured response, appropriate behavior, has all but disappeared in our contemporary culture of instant, disposable celebrity.

Reading through a selection of these letters today can provide a fascinating, wide-angle literary portrait of the entire world during one black weekend a half century ago.

For that world in late November 1963, there were other serious events playing out besides the death of the American president—from military coups in Latin America and Southeast Asia to a deepening ideological split between the two large Communist powers, China and Russia.

For the country, the public embrace of civil rights after August's hugely successful march on Washington was encountering political obstacles in Congress and a backlash in parts of the South. The economy was robust, however, and President Kennedy's prospects for being reelected in 1964 seemed strong. With a larger majority, he might more easily pass his legislative agenda.

For the Kennedys personally, 1963 brought hope, sadness, and surprise. The New Year had found Jackie pregnant with her fourth child (in addition to Caroline and John she'd given birth to a stillborn daughter in

1956). The official announcement was made at Easter, and the baby was due in September. It had been over seventy-five years since a child had been born to a sitting President.

The first of Jacqueline Kennedy's two great tragedies began on August 7, when she went into premature labor. "I don't want anything to happen to this baby," she cried as she was rushed to Otis Air Force Base, where a wing in the base's hospital had been prepared for such an emergency. Patrick Bouvier Kennedy was born six weeks premature, suffering from hyaline membrane disease. The respiratory ailment, which his brother John had been able to overcome, proved too much for the infant, and he died two days later.

The tragedy brought more intimacy and understanding into the marriage. JFK concerned himself with Jackie's recovery. He knew how much she loved the Greek islands and getting away with her sister Lee. When Lee proffered an invitation from Greek shipping tycoon Aristotle Onassis for a two-week Aegean cruise on his yacht *Christina,* Kennedy weighed the benefits to his wife against the political consequences of the First Lady being seen swanning about with Onassis, whose reputation was shady at best. In the end he was adamant she should go.

The trip, which included a stopover in Morocco on the return, worked wonders. Jackie came back to Washington refreshed. Not all problems in the marriage had been resolved, but when JFK casually asked her if she'd agree to accompany him on a political trip the week before Thanksgiving, Jackie opened her red leather Hermès appointment book and, in her spidery handwriting, scrawled "Texas" across November 21, 22, and 23.

One

FOUR DAYS TO REMEMBER

*I*t was the defining moment of a generation. Like the shock of the terrorist attacks of September 11, 2001, the shock of JFK's murder in Dallas on November 22, 1963, stunned and stupefied a nation and the world.

What were you doing when Kennedy was shot? Ask anyone over fifty: For a moment the world seemed to stand still. In factories, offices, coffee shops, and university lecture halls, a pall of disbelief descended. Some students heard the announcement over the PA system in the same classrooms where a year before they'd gone through elaborate drills—hiding under desks in case a nuclear bomb fell nearby. Some teachers and students broke into tears. In Dallas, citizens began to lay wreaths at the site of the fatal shooting, while the publisher of the *Times Herald,* mindful that his city was "sort of on trial," reminded his staff to use the "best of taste" in handling this story.

On one block in the Washington, D.C., suburb of Chevy Chase, a family whose father had helped chart the administration's confrontation with Communism in Southeast Asia waited anxiously as he flew home from a Vietnam War conference in Honolulu. Two doors up the road, the family of the teacher who taught modern-dance classes for Caroline Kennedy and her friends gathered in distress. For this and many other neighborhoods in the capital area, even casual connections with the young couple in the White House had seemed to generate a kind of golden halo. For them, the loss of the President resounded with special force.

That afternoon, an aggrieved silence also seemed to grip many citizens in and around Boston and Cape Cod, where Kennedy had launched his political career. The Catholic Archbishop of Boston, Richard Cardinal Cushing, was speechless before his guest, the city's new naval commander. In Hyannis Port, JFK's mother, Rose, went walking back and forth across the lawn beside the sea, and waited for her youngest son, Teddy, to arrive. She was not even going to try to find the words to describe to her disabled husband what had happened. In Boston's Symphony Hall, conductor Erich Leinsdorf interrupted a concert to make the terrible announcement; the orchestra then played the funeral march from Beethoven's *Eroica* Symphony.

From all across the country and all over the world, telegrams for Mrs. Kennedy poured into the White House well before she returned from Texas. Some came from famous people and world leaders, others from regular citizens. Some offered whatever aid they could. All struggled to give expression to their grief and incomprehension.

❧ *Harold and Dorothy Macmillan, recently resigned British Prime Minister and his wife; thermofax copy*

November 22, 1963

We are numbed by the shock of Jack's death. Nothing we can say can console you. All we can do is to send you our best love.

Harold and Dorothy Macmillan

ᴢ❧ *Konrad Adenauer, former German Chancellor; telegram, in German*

BONN GERMANY 22 2211
MRS JOHN F KENNEDY
   THE INCOMPREHENSIBLE REPORT OF THE DEATH
OF YOUR HUSBAND HAS SHAKEN ME TO THE CORE
IN MOURNING AND HEARTFELT SYMPATHY . . . PRESI-
DENT KENNEDY WILL GO DOWN IN THE HISTORY OF
MANKIND AS A MARTYR FOR FREEDOM AND PEACE
MAY GOD STRENGTHEN YOU
   KONRAD ADENAUER

ᴢ❧ *Donald Rumsfeld, first-term U.S. Congressman from Illinois, future Secre-*
   tary of Defense; telegram

GLENVILLE ILL
MRS. JOHN F KENNEDY
AN INCOMPREHENSIBLE ACT HAS TRAGICALLY ROBBED
YOU YOUR FAMILY AND THE NATION OF A DEDICATED
VALIANT AND SACRIFICING LEADER. IN SHOCKED DIS-
BELIEF AND WITH A DEPTH OF FEELING THAT CANNNOT
BE EXPRESSED I JOIN THE MILLIONS OF MOURNING
PEOPLE ACROSS THE GLOBE IN EXPRESSING MY FAMI-
LYS SORROW AND SYMPATHY AND IN EXTENDING
OUR PRAYERS
DONALD RUMSFELD MEMBER OF CONGRESS

The historic figures of the Democratic Party were quick to express their assurances of aid and comfort, though JFK's rapid rise had often made them uncomfortable. Two-time presidential candidate Adlai Stevenson served loyally as Kennedy's UN Ambassador, but never made a true peace with the young President.

२॰ *Adlai Stevenson, UN Ambassador and former Democratic presidential candidate; telegram*

NEW YORK NY NOV 22 504P EST
MRS JOHN F KENNEDY
I PRAY FOR YOU AND ALL OF US DEVOTEDLY
ADLAI

Harry Truman, originally dismissive of Kennedy on account of his youth, had eventually warmed to the President; his wife sent this card:

२॰ *Bess Wallace Truman, wife of President Harry Truman; undated, engraved card*

Dear Mrs. Kennedy—
I know there is nothing I can say that will give you any comfort but I do want you to know that you have been deeply in my mind and heart through these ghastly days.

Sincerely,
Bess Wallace Truman

Eleanor Roosevelt had also come around to approving of JFK, though she had worked hard to thwart his 1960 nomination in favor of Adlai Stevenson (and had died a year before Kennedy was shot). The Roosevelt children had been more friendly. Franklin Delano Roosevelt Jr. had played a crucial role in JFK's victory in the 1960 West Virginia primary—and later became a good friend of Jackie's. His brother, California congressman James Roosevelt, had refused to take sides in the Stevenson-Kennedy quarrels.

๛ *James Roosevelt, eldest son of Franklin and Eleanor Roosevelt; handwritten note*

> House of Representatives
> Washington, D.C.
> Friday

Dear Jackie;

It is hopeless to say anything that can really help you. Just please know of our affection for you and the children. We want so to do something but just don't know how. We pray of course. God bless you . . . and protect you.

> Jim Roosevelt

In Tulsa, Oklahoma, and Galesburg, Illinois, elementary school children composed letters:

๛ *Brett Ferneau; handwritten letter*

> Nov. 22, 1963

Dear Mrs. Kennedy,

I was terribly shocked when I heard of the cowardly deed some, well, it must been a maniac, performed.

I'm in fourth grade. I was in art when then the news came. One girl started crying. I couldn't bring myself to my senses enough to comfort her, as I was immediately heartsick. I am still heartsick. I am only 9, but I know how great he was. When we went to the library and tried to get a drink, I could only splash water up my nose. I couldn't read, and I didn't hear the teacher when she read a book. I can't express my grief in words.

I give you my deepest sympathy, which I know will not help much, but you may have all I have to give.

This may not be a very good letter but it's the best I can do because I'm still heartsick and I've been writing for almost an hour. As you can see, I still haven't filled the page. I don't think I can.

My sympathy,
Brett Ferneau

Third grade, Douglas School; handwritten letter

Dear Mrs. Kennedy,

We have just heard that President Kennedy died a few minutes ago, and we want to tell you how sad we are.

President Kennedy was a good president and a great man.

Our country will miss him very much.

Sincerely,
The Third Grade
Douglas School
Galesburg, Illinois

In the large corporation in New York City where Ronelle Schneidman worked, she saw "men break down and cry shamelessly in front of their co-workers," while in the streets people "gathered around cars listening to radios. Back home, on Long Island, cars were pulling off the road, drivers too upset to go on." One woman, Barbara Casteen, was out shopping for groceries when she heard the news, as she described in a letter to her parents, later sent on to Mrs. Kennedy.

꙾ *Barbara (Mrs. Charles) Casteen; handwritten letter*

Hyattsville, Maryland
November 27, 1963

Dearest folks:

This has been a long, sad weekend. The silent crowds are gone, the muffled drums are stilled, and the wheels of government begin to grind again. . . .

I think everyone, as long as he lives, will have indelibly stamped upon his memory the exact time and place he happened to be when the news came. I happened to be, of all places, in the supermarket. The loudspeaker was blaring the word that the president had been shot as I walked in the door. Everyone was standing as if frozen to the spot, disbelief and horror on their faces. After a few minutes, I had the presence of mind to get a basket and move along the aisles. . . . As the bulletins came in, people gathered in little knots—strangers, trying to get comfort from each other. Finally, there was a long pause, and the announcer began—"Ladies and gentlemen," and here his voice broke, "The President is dead." There was a gasp, then dead silence. I remember seeing a boy unpacking boxes of cereal, put his head down on an unopened box and weep quietly, his shoulders shaking. Another man, grey-haired and well-dressed, standing at the end of the aisle, his head in his hands, his elbows resting on a stack of Pepsi cartons standing there—unmoved. Ten minutes later he was still standing there. No one talked . . . the horror was too great. All of a sudden I had the urge to get out of there—it seemed incongruous, almost disrespectful, to be there amid the brightness and color, the gay displays. . . . At the checkout counter, the clerk worked mechanically, only his stricken pale face betraying his feelings.

At home, we sat, stunned and transfixed in front of the television. . . .

I think we were waiting for somebody to step in and say it wasn't true, that we were just dreaming. But they never did. . . .

Much love,
Barbara

Despite the shock, citizens expected an orderly transition of power, even in the middle of unfathomable mourning. Within hours the dead President's body was lifted into the rear compartment of Air Force One at Dallas's Love Field. In the front compartment, the new President was sworn in, with JFK's thirty-four-year-old widow at his side. President Johnson asked for the nation's and God's help when he arrived a short while later at Andrews Air Force Base outside Washington. But it was the grieving widow descending from the plane with brother-in-law Bobby who held the attention of the nation. She was still wearing the pink suit that was visibly stained with the blood of her husband. She had refused to change out of it, declaring that "they should see what they have done." For days the obscenity of this spattered skirt would serve as the principal evidence of the bullet's impact; network cameras had not been running at that moment, and amateur film footage of the assassination itself would not emerge for some time.

For the next twenty-four hours, as a heavy rain that perfectly matched the public mood fell over Washington, the nation's collective concern was riveted on Jackie Kennedy. How would she console her children? How, for that matter, would we console our own? Americans were at a loss. One way or another we needed her to give us a cue, to show us what to do. Blessedly, she had an unerring feel for the architecture of social ritual. Under extreme duress, with the help of her brother-in-law and with her children at her side, she showed us how to participate in history as it was created. The funeral she shaped ensured that her husband's greatness would emerge, copying as it did the ceremonies used a century earlier after

Lincoln's assassination: the lying-in-state in the East Room, then in the Capitol Rotunda; the stately procession with the riderless horse; and the burial in Arlington National Cemetery.

She did not compromise the ritual with outbursts of personal emotion, even her own. To the outside world she presented a calm demeanor of silent dignity, breaking down only once in Monday's funeral Mass, shortly before taking communion. It was left to others to make reference to the pathos of the First Lady's personal distress. For example, Mike Mansfield alluded to the intensely personal act of removing her wedding ring and placing it with JFK's body at the hospital in Dallas when, during his Capitol Rotunda eulogy, he intoned repeatedly, at the end of each new sentence: "And so, she took a ring from her finger and placed it in his hands."

Many of the nation's most highly decorated military men paid tribute to the fallen President. "As a former comrade in arms, his death kills

JOHN FITZGERALD KENNEDY
President of the United States
May 29, 1917 – November 22, 1963

✝

Dear God,
Please take care of your servant
John Fitzgerald Kennedy

🙙   🙙   🙙

Now the trumpet summons us again—not as a call to bear arms, though arms we need—not as a call to battle, though embattled we are—but a call to bear the burden of a long twilight struggle, year in and year out, "rejoicing in hope, patient in tribulation"—a struggle against the common enemies of man: tyranny, poverty, disease and war itself . . .

In the long history of the world, only a few generations have been granted the role of defending freedom in its hour of maximum danger. I do not shrink from this responsibility—I welcome it. I do not believe that any of us would exchange places with any other people or any other generation. The energy, the faith, the devotion which we bring to this endeavor will light our country and all who serve it—and the glow from that fire can truly light the world . . .

With a good conscience our only sure reward, with history the final judge of our deeds, let us go forth to lead the land we love, asking His blessing and His help, but knowing that here on earth God's work must truly be our own.

Mass card designed for JFK's funeral.

something within me," General Douglas MacArthur wired the First
Lady in a telegram. Five-star General of the Army Omar Bradley, in the
hospital, sent handwritten regrets that he could not attend the funeral.
Alvin C. York, the legendary hero from the World War I Meuse-Argonne
offensive of 1918, known universally simply as "Sergeant York" since the
1941 Gary Cooper movie of that name, wired a message of "deepest
sympathy and regret." Ill health also prevented Sir Winston Churchill
from attending in person. His grandson wrote from London:

2❧ *Winston Spencer Churchill; handwritten letter*

London
24 November 1963.

Dear Mrs. Kennedy,

   Never have I been so filled with revulsion, anger and sorrow, as when
I heard of your husband's death.

   On this great and good man were set the hopes of humanity. The
grief and loss must be unspeakable for you, who have stood by him
for so many years, and who were at his side when he was struck down.
Nothing can be of consolation to you at this time. But I would like you
to know that throughout the world, and in England especially, all men
who prize Freedom and hope for Peace share your loss and partake of
your grief. . . .

Winston S. Churchill

Shortly after noon on Sunday, many Americans on the East Coast had
just arrived home from intense services at their own houses of worship.
As they turned once more to stare at the television, another act of violence
echoed from Dallas. There, in the crowded basement of the Dallas jail,
a nightclub owner named Jack Ruby had come to exact personal ven-

AMBASSADOR 0770.

11, HYDE PARK GARDENS,
LONDON, W. 2.

24 November 1963.

Dear Mrs. Kennedy,

Never have I been so filled with revulsion, anger and sorrow, as when I heard of your husband's death. On this great and good man were set the hopes of humanity.

. . .

I send you my heart-felt sympathy and deepest affection,

Winston S. Churchill

geance. Friendly with the police, he made his way unremarked into the prison garage where the assassin was being bundled along by a crew of cops, and shot and mortally wounded Lee Harvey Oswald. The killing was caught live on national television hardly forty-eight hours after the murder of the President.

From Dallas the cameras cut back to the hallowed formality of the afternoon's tributes in the Capitol Rotunda. Many of the most important world leaders had already descended on Washington. Several of those who had developed long-lasting relationships with the President had recently left office and did not attend. Harold Macmillan, for example, the

British Prime Minister whose extraordinary sense of humor had earned him a niche in Kennedy's heart unlike that of any other international leader, had resigned in the wake of scandal a mere month earlier. Thus the United Kingdom was represented not by him but by his successor, Sir Alec Douglas-Home.

   Elizabeth and Sir Alec Douglas-Home; message transcribed by U.S. Ambassador David Bruce and transmitted by the British Embassy in Washington

We are horrified by the terrible news and send you our deepest sympathy in your grief.

ELIZABETH AND ALEC DOUGLAS-HOME

Only days before Macmillan left office, the venerable eighty-seven-year-old Chancellor of the German Federal Republic, Konrad Adenauer, had also resigned, paving the way for his former Minister of Economics, Ludwig Erhard, to succeed him. In fact, the White House had been busily preparing for the state dinner honoring the new Prime Minister to take place on Monday, November 25. Instead of being celebrated, Erhard would spend that day paying respects to his would-be host.

   Ludwig Erhard, Chancellor of West Germany; telegram, in German

KOBLENZ 91 22 2340
MRS. JOHN F. KENNEDY
DISTRESSED AND SHAKEN BY THE DEATH OF YOUR HON-
ORABLE PARTNER I TENDER YOU AND YOUR CHILDREN
MY HEARTFELT SYMPATHY FOR THE IRREPLACEABLE LOSS
WHICH HAS OVERTAKEN YOU IN SUCH INCOMPREHENSI-
BLE FASHION IN THIS HEAVY HOUR THE GOVERNMENT

OF THE GERMAN FEDERAL REPUBLIC AND THE ENTIRE
GERMAN PEOPLE FEELS ITSELF CONNECTED TO YOU IN
DEEP MOURNING IN REVERENCE AND THANKFULNESS
WE BOW BEFORE PRESIDENT KENNEDY WHO SHALL
NEVER BE FORGOTTEN AMONG THE GERMAN PEOPLE
LUDWIG ERHARD

Round-the-clock television coverage, free of advertising, continued through Monday's funeral Mass, formal procession, and burial in Arlington National Cemetery. During all of these, Jacqueline Kennedy's self-control allowed viewers to indulge themselves in their identification with her and her children. From California, where news of the President's death hit during the morning hours, came this succinct note of sympathy and acknowledgment:

 Libby (Mrs. Sanford) Byers; handwritten letter

My dear Mrs. Kennedy:
    . . . and still one more wife, mother, teacher, woman, citizen of the United States shares your bereavement.
    Your womanly dignity assists me, as I pray it may sustain you.

Most sincerely,
Libby Byers

One sympathizer who identified with the First Lady—and had discovered the perils of television celebrity for himself when caught up in the quiz show scandals of 1958—was former Columbia University professor Charles Van Doren. He even found a way to pray together with her, despite very different religious beliefs.

Charles Van Doren, onetime contestant on TV's Twenty-One *quiz show; typewritten letter*

New York, NY
November 22, 1963

Dear Mrs. Kennedy:

I am about the age that your husband was when he died, my wife is about your age, I have a daughter who will be six next July, and a son, John, who is a little younger than your John. I call him John-John.

If those things were not true, I would mourn with you on the loss of your President, your friend and your husband. Since they are, I feel almost as if I myself were dead, and were looking on at the mourning for myself, and at the same time were a part of you, and grieving for this loss which is incalculable.

But because the mourning in this family is boundless, the love is also. We love you, all of us, with all of our hearts. In the way that we pray, which is not the same way as you do, formally, we pray for you. May you, as time passes, be peaceful and happy again. And may he be peaceful and rest in whatever happiness there is for the dead. . . .

Yours in utmost sympathy,
Charles Van Doren

Two letters—from a young woman in nearby Virginia and from a family thousands of miles away in the recently admitted state of Alaska—also expressed this identification in poignant terms:

🕬 *Marni Politte; handwritten letter*

Monday, Nov. 25, 1963

Dear Mrs. Kennedy.

Please try to get thru it all—try to be what you have always been. The whole world is mourning and emotional girls like myself have been screaming and crying hysterically thru all of it—but you—the one who has suffered the most—have managed to remain composed. Please don't let anything change that. Remember that the world will love both of you as long as it is filled with human beings. Getting more personal—I always will. Also, if it is possible—think of the children of Lee Harvey Oswald.

Love and respect always,
Marni Politte
Alexandria, Virginia

🕬 *Winfred James Sr. and family; handwritten letter*

Nov. 25th, 1963
Mrs. Jacky Kennedy
Caroline
Jack Jr.
White House Wash. D.C.

We are Eskimo family, located 38 miles away from Eastern Russian coast on the tip of St. Lawrence Island Gambell, Alaska. . . .

Our children . . . all know very much who our dear Mr. President Kennedy is by his voice and by his pictures. They deeply touch me into writing this memory to you and the children especially to Caroline and Jr. whom we tell our children so much. . . . They share with you and your children this morning because they woke me up . . . your time 11am and our time was 5am to listen to the funeral. . . . At this time all the children are up and listening to the rebroadcast with great honor and commiseration.

We live just 50 miles from the Russian Air bases Army bases and missiles bases whom we observe their Jet aircrafts scramble up to air whenever they talk tough until Our Dear Mr. President Kennedy with his great courage backs them away. Seems we see from our village just like when person gets tough and scares little people around and until bigger man show up. Because whenever Mr. President Kennedy challenge them they would back away . . . and we don't see them any more again. That is why we had our greatest respect for him. . . . His leadership during times like Cuban Crises Russian blockade of Berlin roads will never be forgotten. . . .

Our 5 year old daughter Veronica gives her complete sympathy to Caroline. We share in every way with you and the rest of Kennedy family we know very much Our dear Attorney General Robert Kennedy (Ted) Edward Kennedy Mrs. Sargent Shriver and Mr. and Mrs. Joseph P. Kennedy we share with complete feelings of great respect this morning as we are listening to the funeral services thru our radio. We remain

Winfred James, Sr.
and Family

The assassination of 1963 had a special resonance for families who had been through political violence. Rudolf Garfield, great-grandson of President James Garfield, who was fatally wounded by an assassin's bullets in 1881 after serving only four months in office, wrote Mrs. Kennedy about his own "realization of the great personal loss" suffered at the time by his grandfather and great-grandmother. That murder was distant history, but the 1935 murder of populist Louisiana strongman Huey Long was a living memory to members of JFK's generation.

❧ *Russell Long, U.S. Senator from Louisiana, son of populist autocrat Huey Long; typewritten letter*

United States Senate
Washington D.C.
November 23, 1963

Dear Mrs. Kennedy:

Twenty-eight years ago I said my last goodbye to my father who was dying from an assassin's bullet. The intervening years have accorded me the opportunity to meditate about the sort of tragedy which took your husband on Friday.

There is no way to explain such a thing unless one has faith in God and believes in the teachings of Jesus. . . . It is hard to believe that God knows about all of these things and that he planned it to be that way; yet in time we may come to see that all of this is part of a Master plan. . . .

With warmest regards, I am

Sincerely yours,
Russell Long

Memories of the 1930 public funeral in honor of Chief Justice and former President William Howard Taft were evoked in this letter from his granddaughter:

Jackie and her children leave the White House for the funeral. Behind her is Robert Kennedy, flanked by Eunice Kennedy, and in the distance behind them can be seen brother-in-law Peter Lawford. *Abbie Rowe, White House/JFK Library*

≈ *Sylvia Taft Lotspeich, granddaughter of President William Howard Taft; handwritten letter*

November 29

Dear Mrs Kennedy,

A grieving heart compels me to write to you. . . .

We all respond to this tragedy with a common bond of tremendous respect for your husband, admiration for all he has done, and wish that he could have been spared to continue. . . .

Many of us respond with a closer sense of identification because for the first time we were of the same generation as the President. . . . I go back much further in memory to the year I was ten and taken to Washington for the funeral of my grandfather, the other President buried in Arlington cemetery. Your children will also be grateful that they were allowed to take part on Monday.

Sincerely,
Sylvia Taft Lotspeich

In the aftermath of November 22 many Americans clung to the generational promise of JFK's "New Frontier." Many rededicated themselves to fulfilling the late President's vision. The disillusionment and cultural paranoia that would set in after 1965 and the escalation of the war in Vietnam were still far away, but fears of conspiracy and political foul play were there from the very beginning. For the first few hours the Secret Service was suspicious the assassination might be just the first step in a wider conspiracy. Those fears were allayed in the first forty-eight hours, only to be raised again when Jack Ruby shot and killed Lee Harvey Oswald. It was clearly a terrible weekend for James Rowley, the head of the Secret Service, who did not get off a letter of sympathy to the First Lady until Tuesday:

꙳ *James Rowley; typewritten letter*

United States Secret Service
Washington
November 26, 1963

Dear Mrs. Kennedy:

The tragic death of the President has left my associates and me with an indescribable void.

We shall carry on our responsibilities, of course, but with heavy hearts, aware as we are of the irreplaceable loss suffered by you, Caroline and John, and the nation. . . .

We shall always be at your service.

Most sincerely,
James J. Rowley

Others, especially outside the United States, immediately assumed a conspiracy lay behind the killing. Among these was the great French Catholic philosopher Jacques Maritain, who had taught widely in the United States. Maritain's letter to his friend Thomas Merton, written just after Ruby killed Oswald, later became part of the official condolence mail.

≈❧ *Jacques Maritain; handwritten aerogramme, in French*

Toulouse, 25 November 63

My very dear friend,

I was going to write you on account of your article in *Ramparts* . . . when I learned, the day before yesterday, of the assassination of President Kennedy. This news horrified me. Afterwards I thought, in being felled, he has given blood testimony—he, the President of the United States, white, Catholic—victim of racist fanatics. And that this has singular value before God, and that perhaps this will assist the Christian conscience to reveal itself, to hold itself ready for the historic *Kairos*.

Now I am reading today's papers. The fact that the presumed assassin has been killed confirms the impression of its being a racial crime—that its authors seek to camouflage it as a Communist attack: the same sort of plot as Hitler's when he set fire to the Reichstag. Thus the true significance of the assassination of the President will be hidden, the Blacks will not know that he has fallen *for them,* the moment for the Whites to awake will be lost. Yet it seems to me impossible the investigation will not reveal the truth.

. . . My heart turns to you because of the love I have for you and for your country. . . .

I embrace you
Jacques

Back in Dallas, those whose lives had been caught up in Friday's tragedy tried to sort out its many meanings. Judge Sarah T. Hughes, who on Friday afternoon administered the oath of office to Lyndon B. Johnson on Air Force One while Jacqueline Kennedy looked on, wrote, "Your courage at the ceremony . . . will always be an inspiration for me." Sister Rosemary O'Donohue had taken a break from her job at St. Paul's Hospital to see the President up close. She wrote about her experience to her parents, who forwarded the letter to Mrs. Kennedy:

≈ *Sister Rosemary O'Donohue; typewritten letter*

My dearest Mamma and Daddy:

. . . It was a wonderful thrill and experience to be among a crowd of so many people brought together to welcome the Kennedys to Dallas. . . . At about 10:45 it stopped raining and the sky was a beautiful blue with pretty white clouds. . . . Soon the motorcade was coming down the street and then we saw the two of them. He looked so darling and he had a real wide smile and his eyes were real bright and wrinkles along side of his eyes due to the big smile and oh he just looked grand. And Mrs. Kennedy was real darling too . . . big smile, and her graceful wave. We were so close to them that if I wanted to, I could have reached out and touched the car. Just as they came near to the spot where we were standing they looked over on the other side at young school children all lined up for them. But soon he caught sight of us and turned toward us and waved and said "Oh the Sisters." Then it was over all too soon. We beat it back to the car and drove over to the Dallas Trade Mart so that we could get another look at them in real life before they entered into the Mart for dinner. But as we turned up the drive of the Mart we saw the motorcade right in front of us and racing toward Parkland Hospital. No one knew what or why. . . . Then a young girl poked her head in the window and said that the President had been shot.

Rosemary

Dallas police officer J. D. Tippit was killed by Lee Harvey Oswald less than an hour after the assassination. Tippit was patrolling the area near Oswald's rooming house in his cruiser when he spotted the suspect and stopped him, only to be cut down by Oswald's revolver in front of several eyewitnesses. Fleeing the scene on foot, Oswald rushed into the Texas Theater several blocks away without buying a ticket; the ticket taker alerted the police, who arrived to take custody of the double murderer. Tippit was the thirty-nine-year-old father of three, a decorated World War II veteran, with eleven years' experience on the Dallas police force. His widow telegrammed Mrs. Kennedy hours later:

2❧ *Marie Tippit; telegram*

MAY I ADD MY SYMPATHY TO THAT OF PEOPLE ALL OVER THE WORLD. MY PERSONAL LOSS IN THIS GREAT TRAGEDY PREPARES ME TO SYMPATHIZE MORE DEEPLY WITH YOU.
MRS. J. D. TIPPIT DALLAS TEXAS

The night of the assassination, Marie Tippit received phone calls from both Bobby Kennedy and Lyndon Johnson; from the White House, spe-

cial presidential assistant Arthur Schlesinger wrote her a personal note at
the First Lady's request. A few weeks after the deaths of their husbands,
Jacqueline Kennedy sent the Dallas widow a photograph of the Kennedy
family taken the previous Easter at Joe Kennedy's house in Palm Beach,
inscribed "There is another bond we share. We must remind our children
all the time what brave men their fathers were."

Among the political purposes of the Dallas trip had been to present a united Democratic Party front as a counter to the widely chroni-
cled feud between the state's top two Democrats, Governor John
Connally and Senator Ralph Yarborough. Governor Connally, who
had been riding in the same car with the Kennedys, suffered serious
wounds in the chest and thigh but was saved in the operating room at
Parkland Hospital. Yarborough had been riding in the second car with
the Johnsons, and was unhurt. All day Saturday Governor Connally
lay heavily guarded and half-comatose in Parkland Hospital, only
learning after much muddled prodding of his wife, Nellie, "the full
truth"—that Kennedy had been killed. In a telegram sent on Sunday
John and Nellie Connally offered prayers for both the President's
widow and all Americans. Senator Yarborough and his wife had struck
a similar note in their joint telegram to Jacqueline Kennedy sent a day
earlier.

❧ *Texas Senator Ralph Yarborough; telegram*

NOVEMBER 23
WE SEND OUR DEEPEST AND LASTING SYMPATHY TO
YOU, YOUR CHILDREN AND YOUR FAMILY . . . AND . . .
PRAY THAT A MERCIFUL PROVIDENCE WILL ASSUAGE
YOUR GRIEF, AND STRENGTHEN YOU FOR YOUR TASKS
AHEAD.
RALPH AND OPAL YARBOROUGH

The events of the terrible weekend had cast a deep shadow over Dallas. On Monday the twenty-fifth at a special memorial service at Wynnewood Baptist Church, the Reverend Ray S. Brown put into words what many had been asking: "What has happened to our city?" He declared that it was "time for us each and all to reexamine ourselves and our attitudes."

Many speakers at memorial services around the country that day echoed a similar theme. In an evocative eulogy at the Solemn Requiem Mass held for President Kennedy in the Church of St. Francis Xavier in Manhattan, Reverend Anthony S. Woods, S.J., observed that "the world is bent . . . down low with shock, grief, anguish because it somehow senses that something has happened in our country which is, as far as I can see, of the nature of a sacrilege." Edgar M. Carlson, president of Gustavus Adolphus College in St. Peter, Minnesota, asked why we "cannot protect [our] own president against lawless violence at home," and alluded to the recent refusal by the governors of Alabama and Mississippi to obey Federal Court desegregation orders, asking whether "there may not be some relation between the defiance of law and order . . . by communities and states, and the defiance of law and order by individuals."

More skeptical voices were sharp in discussing what they perceived as southern bigotry. An anonymous citizen from York, Pennsylvania, penned a string of verses entitled "And They Took the Yankee Home," built around the YANKEE, GO HOME sign seen in the crowd that morning in Dallas. And much press coverage focused on incidents of right-wing heckling that preceded the assassination, and some reports of satisfaction that followed it.

But as Thanksgiving 1963 approached, most voices around the country tried to move the conversation toward common goals. One of the more eloquent Thanksgiving addresses that reached Mrs. Kennedy came from the Ambassador to Jordan, career diplomat William Macomber, a man who had fought with the French Resistance and later became president of an institution very dear to the former First Lady, the Metropolitan Museum of Art.

🌒 *Ambassador William Macomber; typed speech sent with handwritten note*

American Community Thanksgiving Service
November 28, 1963

My fellow Americans,

For all of us, the past few days have been almost indescribably sad. . . .

We mourn the loss of an intensely human and attractive person— the first president born in this century—and an ornament to our time and era.

We . . . cannot really believe that at the age of 46 this man . . . is no more.

And gone with him, too, are so many other of his qualities which we so much admired:

His undeniable capacity for leadership,

his zest for his job,

his gallantry, charm, gaiety, and humor

his way with words,

his Lincolnesque self-confidence combined in that strange Lincolnesque manner with genuine and affable humility,

his ability to lift up our hearts,

and above all, his reassuringly courageous conviction that through sacrifice, wisdom and steadfastness an enduring and just world peace may yet be achieved. . . .

Yet as I speak to you today I am mindful of a further quality . . . a sense of perspective . . . most often expressed in a few casual Boston-accented words—and an accompanying grin.

And today I am sure he would want us to retain our own perspective, too . . . to remember that, despite our grief, we still do have much to stop, and to consider, and to be thankful for. . . .

Two

FAMILY AND CLOSE FRIENDS

*O*ver the years, the Kennedys had come to be regarded as a kind of American dynasty: a family you either loved or hated, but could not ignore. Jacqueline Kennedy was unlike any of her in-laws, but she had become indissolubly associated with them over the ten-year roller coaster of her marriage, conducted in the glare of national politics.

Of all Jack's siblings, the one Jacqueline trusted most was Bobby. Jack's campaign manager, Attorney General, and closest counselor was also the one she could count on in a pinch. He had been there for her after her miscarriage in 1956, when Jack was still off on a sailing trip. Now, moments after the aircraft taxied into place at Andrews Air Force Base the evening of November 22, Bobby slipped through the front entrance of the plane while its ramp was still rolling into place. He rushed through the aircraft and appeared as if magically at Jackie's side in the rear of Air Force One.

A suite had been taken at Bethesda Naval Hospital to accommodate the party of mourners while the autopsy was carried out. The ambulance-hearse headed there, with Jackie and Bobby sitting in back with the

President's coffin. Already she had refused to change clothes or be separated prematurely from Jack, and now again she refused the helicopter offered: She would stay with the body.

Bobby had heard the news at home in McLean, Virginia, at Hickory Hill, the house owned by Jack when he was a senator. The Kennedys were practiced at dealing with tragedy, if not grief, and third brother Bobby immediately stepped into a role similar to that taken on by Jack when his own older brother, Joe, had died during World War II. Bobby was more intense than his older brother—more religious and less ironic. And now there was also more riding on his shoulders: Not only was he Attorney General, but his father, Joseph P. Kennedy, onetime Ambassador to the United Kingdom and the architect of the family's public success, had been an invalid since suffering a massive stroke in December 1961. No one but Bobby could step in to fill the shoes as head of the family.

Immediately Bobby had started making arrangements for his brothers and sisters. Younger brother Ted, who as junior Senator from Massachusetts had been presiding over the Senate when the first report came, was assigned the task of flying to Hyannis Port to break the news in person to their ailing father; their sister Eunice would accompany him to the Cape. Sister Pat Lawford was at home in Los Angeles. Jean Smith, the Kennedy sister who felt closest to Jackie, would fly immediately from New York to Washington to be with the First Lady, while brother-in-law Stephen would switch assignments—from preparations for the 1964 presidential reelection campaign to preparations for the lying-in-state and funeral, along with Eunice's husband, Peace Corps director Sargent Shriver.

In the first hour after news of the President's death, sympathizers began to turn up at Bobby's home. They included Nicole Alphand, wife of the French Ambassador, whose picture had appeared on the cover of *Time* magazine on newsstands that week, dated November 22. Her husband, Hervé, was the senior member of the Washington Diplomatic Corps. The proper thing to do, she felt, beyond sending a telegram to the First Lady, was to make a personal call on the family.

2❧ *Hervé Alphand, French Ambassador, and his wife, Nicole; telegram, in French*

WASHINGTON DC 22 401P
MRS. JOHN F KENNEDY
   DEVASTATED BY THE NEWS OF THE TRAGIC DEATH OF PRESIDENT JOHN F. KENNEDY, I OFFER THE EX- PRESSION OF OUR MOST SORROWFUL CONDOLENCES IN THE NAME OF NICOLE AND MYSELF. THE PRESI- DENT . . . AND YOU HAVE ALWAYS KEPT THE MOST OPEN AND MARKED WELCOME TOWARDS NICOLE AND ME, FRIENDLY FEELINGS WHICH WE SHALL FOREVER CHERISH IN MEMORY.
   ALLOW ME TO TELL YOU HOW DEEPLY WE ARE SHAKEN BY THE IRREPARABLE LOSS THAT HAS HIT YOU, YOURS, AND YOUR COUNTRY. OUR THOUGHTS ARE WITH YOU . . . HERVE AND NICOLE ALPHAND

Rose Fitzgerald Kennedy was the undisputed matriarch of the Kennedy clan. Daughter of Boston's onetime mayor "Honey Fitz" Fitzgerald, she had practice leaning on her strict but deep Catholic faith to guide her through family tragedies. She heard the news when her husband's care- taker, alerted by a maid, suddenly turned up the volume on a television set. Immediately, all television sets in the Hyannis Port house were turned off so that Joe would not hear about the tragedy from an imper- sonal source. Teddy would not arrive for a few hours; in any event, Rose believed that the bad news should wait until the morning.

Rose Fitzgerald and Joseph P.
Kennedy Sr. *Family Collection
Archives, JFK Library*

Other close associates of the
Kennedys would find out in
shocking and sometimes even
rude ways. Just how unexpected
the events of November 22 were
to those around the President is
illustrated graphically by the
correspondence that reached
JFK's secretary, Evelyn Lincoln,
from Evelyn Jones, one of the
loyal Kennedy employees at
their Palm Beach home. The
President had stayed there dur-
ing his visit to Florida the weekend before traveling to Texas. In a cover
letter dated November 22, Ms. Jones talks about "the President's night
shirts & white jersey & one silver teaspoon" left behind after the recent
stopover and encloses a bill for four days of cleaning and laundry. The second letter, dated three days later, comes from another universe of concern
altogether.

ᘍ *Evelyn Jones; handwritten letter*

Nov. 25, 1963

Dear Mrs. Lincoln
I am heartsick over the President's death. . . .
I had just finished a letter to you enclosing a bill . . . and had planned

to mail it on my way home on Friday when I learned the news. I have been unable to even send it but will enclose it with this. . . . Just ignore the part about the pictures & I'm holding the package of clothes until I can find out what to do with them. . . .

Please convey my deep sympathy to Mrs. John Kennedy and I am going to try to write to her soon . . . Both Caroline & John are indeed blessed to call her "Mother."

I received word Friday afternoon bluntly over the phone from a Miami reporter. . . . I took the call in the office & I just sat down in the chair with the phone in my hand & then hung up.

I still have not recovered from the shock. . . . Naturally I have also been worrying about its effect on Mr. Kennedy Sr. I know it is going to be a difficult season but maybe those of us who know & love them can ease the pain just a little.

Please also give my sincere sympathy to all of the members of the Secret Service & tell them I know that it may seem to them they failed the President, but he would be the first to deny it, because he knew as we do they loved him & would lay down their life for him had it been God's will. . . .

I am proud to have known you & all of the others. . . .

> Gratefully yours,
> Evelyn Jones

Though the bulk of the condolence mail flew into White House mailboxes, the other Mrs. Kennedy, JFK's mother, was not neglected. Among the letters Rose Kennedy received was one from Pat Skakel Cuffe, the older sister of her daughter-in-law Ethel, and the first of the Skakel girls in whom Bobby Kennedy had taken a romantic interest, but who had gone on to marry an Irishman and settle in Dublin.

❧ *Pat Skakel Cuffe, Bobby Kennedy's sister-in-law; handwritten letter to Mrs. Joseph P. Kennedy Sr.*

County Dublin

Dear Mrs. Kennedy,

All through these terrible days I grieve for you and Mr. Kennedy—stunned at the measure of your sorrow.—I hope it will be of some joy to

CARRIC GOLLIGAN
QUARRY ROAD, SHANKILL
COUNTY DUBLIN

Dear Mrs. Kennedy,

All Through these terrible days I grieve for you and Mr. Kennedy— stunned at The measure of your sorrow. — I hope

. . .

No one is prouder. Than I am to share his citizenship, his Faith,— and Through Ethel and Patty,— his family. —

love,

Pat Skakel Cuffe

you to know that surely every person in Ireland has prayed for your son today—and for his splendid family. The memory of the Irish being what it is, you will be prayed for on this island for years and years to come. . . . Schools and shops, government and business is at a standstill today . . . Only Jack could have so caught the respect and love of a country not his own.

No one is prouder than I am to share his citizenship, his Faith, and through Ethel and Bobby,—his family.—

love,

Pat Skakel Cuffe

The President's own children had to be told as well. Their mother felt in too much shock to handle it in the first hours afterward, so the task passed to their nanny, Maud Shaw. Miss Shaw believed, at least in Caroline's case, that the news should *not* wait until morning. Caroline, just shy of her sixth birthday, cried herself to sleep. John Jr. would turn three on Monday, November 25, the day of his father's funeral. Despite explanations from his mother, uncles, and others, he seemed to remain mystified by his father's disappearance.

In Georgetown, Jackie's mother, Janet Auchincloss, found out when the First Lady's social secretary, Nancy Tuckerman, called her from the White House. Janet was used to standing in for her daughter at White House social functions, but the next few days would strain even her usually placid demeanor. Before she could contact her daughter, the wife of the Peruvian Ambassador dropped by the house to offer condolences. The Secret Service wanted to get Caroline and John Jr. out of the White House, so they brought the children and their nanny to their grandmother's house, while Janet and her husband, Hugh, the First Lady's stepfather, headed first to the Executive Mansion, then to Bethesda to await her daughter's return with the President's body.

While military doctors conducted the autopsy downstairs in the Naval Hospital's morgue, Jacqueline Kennedy and a few family members and friends gathered in the seventeenth-floor VIP suite. Fourteen years earlier, Truman's Secretary of Defense, James Forrestal, had committed suicide while hospitalized for depression in the VIP suite one floor below. Forrestal had mentored young John Kennedy on foreign affairs during a European tour shortly after World War II, and his son Michael was a key Kennedy foreign policy aide. In a brief note to the First Lady two days later Forrestal's widow, Josephine, wrote: "No need to tell you I've some clue to how you must be feeling."

As the mourning party stood there in shock on this bleak November night, Jackie alternated between offering thoughtful, personal words of consolation to a family or close staff member and replaying the trauma at Dealey Plaza in an explosive stream of words and memories. Some calm and comfort seemed to come in stretches she spent with Bob McNamara and her brother-in-law in the little kitchen of the suite, telling and retelling the details of those terrible moments, as if purging herself of them. Much of the time, though, Bobby was coordinating arrangements for the funeral and ceremonies, often with a team back at the White House that included his brother-in-law Sargent Shriver and presidential speechwriters and advisers Richard Goodwin and Arthur Schlesinger. As the waiting period dragged on, some family members tried to catch a few minutes' sleep. It wasn't until after four A.M. Saturday that the grieving party arrived home for the night and the casket was lifted onto the catafalque in the East Room of the White House.

Though attention inevitably focused on Jack Kennedy's family, the President's death was also shattering for his in-laws. Jackie's relationship with her own family had been complicated by divorce and remarriage, but her Bouvier inheritance was strong, and the Auchincloss connection was a continuing source of stability. Among the messages of condolence streaming toward the First Lady were those from her own relations. Jackie's flamboyantly bohemian, big-hearted Aunt Edith and extravagant first cousin Edie, who had long since fallen on hard times, sent a telegram from their dilapidated East Hampton home, Grey Gardens:

❧ *Aunt Edith Bouvier and her daughter, "Little Edie" Beale; telegram*

MRS JOHN F KENNEDY
  BETHESDA NAVAL HOSPITAL
   EDIE AND I SEND OUR DEEPEST SYMPATHY AT THIS TRAGIC HOUR JACK WAS THE GREATEST PRESIDENT THE UNITED STATES WILL EVER HAVE OUR PRAYERS ARE SAID FOR YOU AND THE FAMILY
YOUR AUNT EDITH BOUVIER AND EDIE BEALE

A few hours after the body came home to 1600 Pennsylvania Avenue, members of the disparate wings of the First Couple's family started converging there. Despite the impending separation and divorce of the Hollywood branch of the Kennedys, Patricia and Peter Lawford made a special effort to arrive in Washington together. Jackie's sister Lee Radziwill, her only regular confidante during the White House years, was on her way from London aboard the earliest jet she could book. Her stepfather Hugh Auchincloss's son Yusha, who had spent memorable teenage years together with Jackie, was there. So was a single member of the Bouvier clan: the sister of her beloved departed father, "Black Jack" Bouvier, Maude Davis. The Bouvier relative closest to Jackie, her godfather, Michel Bouvier III, or "Miche," sent a strong telegram of sympathy and love from Paris, where he was living with his wife and two sons. Jackie herself was the godmother of the younger son, John Vernou Bouvier IV, or "Jayvie," named after her father.

The Kennedy cousins were more numerous than the Bouviers. Telegrams with a Kennedy family connection would arrive from Maryland, West Virginia, Rhode Island, and Upstate New York; from distant cousins in England and Ireland; and from "the brother of the priest who sent the Irish wolfhound to the White House." Mary Ann Ryan, Kennedy's distant cousin from Dunganstown, County Wexford, with whom he had recently reconnected, even showed up from Ireland in time for the funeral and to be introduced to Jackie at the reception that took place afterward at the White House. From Florida came words of commiseration and consolation from JFK's aunt Loretta, his father's sister, and from his cousin Mary Lou McCarthy, who had played with the younger Kennedys during summers at Hyannis Port and briefly did charity work with JFK's sister Eunice in Chicago.

❧ *Loretta (Mrs. George) Donnelly; telegram*

ST. AUGUSTINE FLO NOV 23
DEAREST JACQUELINE MAY GODS LOVE AND THE WORLDS PRAYERS SUSTAIN YOU STOP I TOO AM HEARTBROKEN LOVE AUNT LORETTA

❧ *Mary Lou McCarthy; handwritten letter*

Nov. 24, 1963

Dearest Jacqueline,

I loved your Jack too! God grant you the strength to carry on. Looking through our Bible tonight I found something which may help you.

From the Book of Wisdom: "But the just man, though he die early, shall be at rest. For the age that is honorable comes not with the passing of time, nor can it be measured in terms of years. Having become perfect in a short while, he reached the fullness of a long career; for his soul was pleasing to the Lord, therefore he sped him out of the midst of wickedness. But the people saw and did not understand; nor did they take into account that God's grace and mercy are with his holy ones and his care is with his elect."

Our prayers are with you, Caroline and little John, Aunt Rose and Uncle Joe.

with love,
Mary Lou Connelly McCarthy

From the family line of Ambassador Joe's other sister, Margaret Kennedy Burke, came words of a distant cousin, an adolescent girl:

?♥ *Brigid Kennedy, niece of JFK's cousin Marnie; handwritten letter*

East Aurora, New York
Dear Mrs. Kennedy,

I am the niece of Mrs. John Devine (Marnie Burke), the President's cousin. I would like you to know how grief stricken I am at the news of your husband. I was never so shocked. . . . In all my 12 years on this earth November 22 is the saddest of my life.

Truly this event is a national disgrace. . . . to think that our nation that is supposed to be so "civilized" has done this to such a man. . . .

Let me say this much Mrs. Kennedy I have never seen any woman undergo misfortune as this with the courage and grace you have shown. . . .

I am a seventh grade pupil. . . . Soon I hope to hunt a horse of my own. But that is besides the point. I sympathize with you. May God Bless You.

Sincerely,
Brigid Kennedy

Another youth closer to hand was thirteen-year-old Craig McNamara, son of the Secretary of Defense, who came with his parents during the Cabinet's viewing of the bier. Bringing sons and daughters (Arthur Schlesinger's children came as well) was not surprising, given the late President's interest in his associates' families.

    ✌ *Craig McNamara, son of Robert and Marjorie McNamara; handwritten letter*

Dear Mrs. Kennedy,

We are all grieved at the death of President Kennedy. He was one of the most wonderful men in the history of the United States.

I could never express the feeling I had toward the President and all the wonderful things he did for his country.

It has been a privilege for the McNamara family to be part of the cabinet.

May God give you, Caroline and John all the courage in the world. My deepest regards to you.

Love,

Craig McNamara

As Jacqueline Kennedy turned her attention to the upcoming ceremonies for her husband, she could rely at least partly on her own experience: Five years earlier when her father had died, she had immediately stepped in to make arrangements. Sunday evening, while much of the family wing upstairs at the White House rang with loud Irish song—the Kennedys' antidote to brooding depression—Jackie single-mindedly made lists and relayed instructions to Bobby and others. She had inherited from her father a sense of being special, and from her mother a taste for privacy.

They would serve her well in the chaotic whirl of the assassination's aftermath.

Many of Jackie's Washington social friends lent a helping hand. Hostess and socialite Florence Mahoney dropped off fresh caviar and homemade bread with a message that noted: "so good cut thru and toasted." Despite the Kennedy family's push for a burial in Brookline or Boston, Jackie argued for nearby Arlington National Cemetery, and enlisted McNamara, Bobby, her sisters-in-law Pat and Jean, and other close Kennedy associates to support the idea. Despite the Church hierarchy's wish for a requiem Mass in the large, opulent National Shrine, she insisted it be held at St. Matthew's Cathedral, within walking distance of the White House. She remembered JFK's affection for the bagpipers of the Black Watch Regiment and how moved he had been on his June trip to hear the Irish mourning drill played for fallen warriors; both the Scottish bagpipers and Irish cadets played an essential role in the ceremonies.

When Monday came, the funeral Jackie had devised in the midst of her distress perfectly suited the pageantry of the occasion. Her sense of poise surprised even her family. "I never saw her cry, even in the White House," her stepbrother Yusha Auchincloss recalled. Chuck Spalding, a longtime friend of Jack Kennedy's from his early days in Washington, was forthright in his admiration:

ᴈ☙ *Charles Spalding; handwritten note*

Dear Jackie

The day reached the required level—and then went beyond it. You were a hero's wife—and beyond it.

I'm near if you need anything.

Chuck

A letter composed right after the funeral by Wendy Burden Morgan, a Virginia neighbor of the Auchinclosses and the Robert Kennedys and wife of ABC radio commentator Edward P. Morgan, reflects the intense feelings of a long friendship.

❧ *Wendy (Mrs. Edward P.) Morgan; handwritten letter*

Monday evening

Dearest Jackie—

I write you in an anguish that cannot be expressed . . .

Your cry of "Oh, no" wells up in me, over and over as I am still unable to accept this hideous tragedy. . . .

Saturday night, walking through those magnificent rooms which you have made so beautiful and are in such a real sense "yours," I was overwhelmed by the beauty and simplicity you had directed—and the intolerable agony of this thing for you.

Your courage and bearing through these days have been truly inspired and it is the same brand of courage that your brilliant, staunch, gay husband possessed. Despite this torment of shocking loss, you are finishing your job as a President's wife with the same beauty and dignity you have shown throughout—and my admiration knows no bounds. . . .

I praise God for only two things at this moment. First, that you were with him. . . . And second, that he was here long enough to comfort you through the loss of your baby and grew closer to you than I somehow feel he had ever been before.

Your two ravishing children have so shattered the emotions of all of us by their young gallantry and grace—and by the knowledge of what a wonderful, glowing father they will now have to do without. . . .

Please God that you may find somewhere, in time, a new life which is a happy one—a world apart from what you have had, with its burdens, privileges and recent agony—but which will be fulfilling and lovely.

Bless you, bless you—through this black time. . . .

Wendy—

During the Thanksgiving weekend that followed the funeral, Jacqueline Kennedy retreated from the glare of twenty-four-hour media coverage to Hyannis Port. Tens of thousands of Americans wrote to her that day, some of them good friends.

❧ *Mr. and Mrs. James D. Hurd, Washington friends; handwritten letter*

28-XI-63

Dear Jackie:

We send a few words of condolence having lived in the sunlight and sudden shadow of a man. . . . A man undiminished by death. A man magnified by your love.

Now the love transfers. The President gave "that we might give of ourselves, that we might give to one another until there would be no room, no room at all," for this to happen again in our country. . . .

On Thanksgiving Day, as all this past week, our hearts turn to you. . . .

James and Nancy
(Mr. & Mrs. James D. Hurd)

Jazz pianist, journalist, and Sinatra biographer Robin Douglas-Home, who was a few years younger than Jackie, had several personal conversations with her during a vacation she shared with Lee and the kids in Ravello, Italy, and at the Kennedys' new country house on Rattlesnake Mountain, in Virginia.

≈ *Robin Douglas-Home, friend; handwritten letter*

3 December 63

My dear Jackie,

I have not written before this on purpose. For obvious reasons. I could only send out thought-waves to you through the atmosphere and hope you received them. You know what I would have said in those thought-waves, and it is better to leave them as thoughts, unspoken and unwritten. For to speak or to write them would be superfluous and serve only to devalue them, and the emotion they would try to describe.

Everything you said that evening at Rattlesnake kept coming back to me. I remember mainly you saying: "Don't, don't, *ever* get bitter." Now it sounds so ironic, coming from you who have so much you could be bitter about, to me who has, by comparison, nothing. But one thing I know— that it will never be necessary for anyone to say those words to you.

I am prouder than ever to know you as I do. And to feel about you as I do. You are someone very special: you have always been special to me. Now you are special in the eyes of the world. I only wish that the world could have remained blind, and that the tragedy could have turned into the nightmarish dream I still want to wake up and find it really was.

love
Robin

Close friends and family worried about the First Lady in the weeks after the assassination. Some knew from visits to her in the Georgetown town house she borrowed from Averill and Pamela Harriman afterward that she remained devastated, and encouraged her to get away; she and her two children would, in fact, spend the Easter holiday in Antigua with sister Lee and her husband, as well as brother-in-law Bobby and Chuck Spalding.

🐿 *Robert P. Cramer, longtime political associate of JFK; handwritten letter*

Virgin Islands Corporation
St. Croix, Virgin Islands

Dear Jackie,

I wish I had the expression to tell you how terribly we miss Jack. We loved him. He was the greatest. We are privileged to have been able to work for him.

Sally, Robby and I came to the White House for the funeral. We wanted so much to express our sympathies to you and the children, but it just didn't seem to be the right time to interrupt. We do so now.

Unfortunately, we must somehow accept although never quite understand what has happened during these recent tragic days. However, they give me an even stronger indication that there has to be a purpose and a pattern for both life and death. . . .

It is warm and quiet here. We have lots of room and would love to see you—with or without the children. . . .

Bob

🐿 *Michael Canfield, former husband of Jackie's sister Lee; handwritten letter*

Jan. 6th

Dearest Jackie—

I am so sad to think of your sadness, and sad again to know that Jack and I shall meet nevermore. I liked him enormously.

I do hope that some day we may see you here.

Love, as always—
Michael

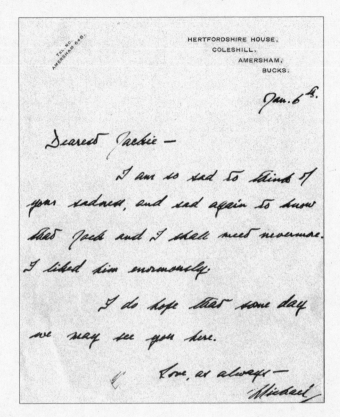

HERTFORDSHIRE HOUSE,
COLESHILL,
AMERSHAM,
BUCKS.

Jan. 6th.

Dearest Jackie —

I am so sad to think of your sadness; and sad again to know that Jack and I shall meet nevermore. I liked him enormously.

I do hope that some day we may see you here.

Love, as always —

Michael

James A. Reed, old friend of JFK's from their PT boat days who also served as Assistant Secretary of the Treasury; handwritten letter

January 8, 1964

Dear Jackie—

Of course, I have been thinking a great deal of you and the children. I wish I could be of some solace to you; and indeed, as you know, I would be most happy to help you in any way that I can.

I hope that this finds you and the children well. While the Christmas season must have been most difficult for you, I trust that the change of scene and the climate had a salutary effect.

I hope to see you soon and with every good wish—

Affectionately,

Jim

Three

MEMORIES

*A*midst the thousands of letters that arrived from family, friends, leaders, artists, and celebrities were also many that contained personal recollections about the slain president. Jacqueline Kennedy had let it be known that she was interested in these reminiscences; neighbors, schoolmates, teachers, friends, associates, and passing acquaintances responded willingly to her request. So did thousands of fans and well-wishers who had no more personal connection than shaking hands with or waving at the late President.

Some of these letters contain memories of encounters with Jack at any one of his several childhood homes. One group revolves around the Kennedy kids' Hyannis Port adventures. Cyril Carpenter Smith, a school supervisor then in the Hyannis area, recalled going "sharking" on a friend's yacht in the late 1920s and taking the ten- or twelve-year-old Jack Kennedy along for a "fine sail in the Sound"; the sailors "kept only the shark's teeth for souvenirs." Ramona Chaffin recalled becoming chummy over the phone with several of the young Kennedys while working as a telephone operator in Hyannis and once missing a chance to spend the evening at the

Kennedy house with Bobby. Perhaps the most philosophical of childhood recollections came from a former Brookline and Hyannis Port neighbor:

 Esther Edwards; handwritten letter

Milton, Massachusetts

December 31, 1963

Dear Mrs. Kennedy,

. . . I wanted to write you, too, because I am a neighbor of yours at Hyannis Port, though I've only been there in snatches in recent summers. But as a child I played with Jack and Joe there—though "battled" is perhaps a more accurate description of what we usually did. Moreover, we lived very close to their house in Brookline in the winters, too, for the first dozen years of our lives. Almost the first people I can remember other than my immediate family were Joe and Jack. Life was never . . . dull around them.

To get to my special friend's house to play there was a dreadful choice of running the gauntlet by some terrifying wasps . . . or going by the Kennedys' house. I remember being "captured" by Joe and Jack as I rode by on my tricycle, aged I suppose five, Joe a little older, Jack younger, and being shut solemnly in their garage. I remember sitting there . . . paralyzed with fright—a stripe of sun on the cement floor, the voices of children playing outside, and a sense of utter loneliness, the feeling that I would never get home again (. . . all of half a block away). Finally, nothing further happening, I crept out, astonished to be alive and unchased.

I remember a tremendous black eye I got, *circa* eight, by being pulled out of a tree on my head by Joe and Jack. I'm sure I remember it because I was proud of it! I remember too being chased by the two boys down a snowy street, frightened but feeling even in full flight that this time it was just—they were defending valiantly their nursemaid, who I had just rashly said, had a nose like a turnip! . . .

I remember the summer your family first came to Hyannis Port. I was walking up the pier, aged eight or so, rejoicing in the lovely vista and summer ahead—when there on the beach just at the head of the pier I spied two familiar small boys. At home in Brookline we would have sprung to arms instantly, but in a new setting and all of us at the moment lacking playmates, we greeted each other with at least muted enthusiasm. There followed probably the longest truce of our childhoods, which finally terminated in a great naval battle in row boats. . . .

I wish I knew now why there was so much conflict between us. . . . It doesn't matter now, except as a foil for what came afterwards.

When Jack ran for President, I remembered all too clearly the aggressiveness and the will to dominate of the child. I questioned in my mind his ability to handle the overwhelming power of the office. Would he be tempted in a crisis to use that power to overwhelm opposition, in a destructive way . . . ?

What I saw was the true wonder of the growth that had intervened. The small boy whose heart had been set on winning without much regard for his opponent's rights . . . had become the man who could use power wisely, magnanimously, for peace and justice for all mankind. The old strength of will was there—but tempered with understanding and concern for others. This was in truth a glorious victory, a victory of mind and heart and character. . . .

He was a good and great man, through inward growth and achievement as much as through outward power and position. Perhaps when one's childhood foe can say this, in deep respect and loving appreciation, it is about as complete an accolade as can be granted. . . .

Sincerely,
Esther Edwards

The Kennedy children were sent to private day and boarding schools; their mother and father were often traveling elsewhere. At age seven Jack Kennedy was transferred from Catholic school to the well-established preparatory school Noble & Greenough, whose primary wing was located in Brookline. Two years later when "Nobles" dissolved its primary division, Joseph Kennedy played an instrumental role in forming the Dexter School to take its place. In his note to Jacqueline Kennedy of November 22, 1963, Dexter's then headmaster, Francis Caswell, recounted that earlier in the day the whole school had observed a "period of prayerful silence" in the very gymnasium where Jack and his older brother had played as young boys.

JFK spent his most formative adolescent years at the Choate School in Wallingford, Connecticut—the elite boarding school his older brother, Joe, already attended. Ed Van Dyke, a Choate student who lived a few doors down the hall from the room shared by Jack and Joe, recalled in his letter to Jacqueline Kennedy the brothers' popularity and roughhousing, and Jack's quick wit. They also "seemed to be the only 'boys' at Choate that knew F.D.R. would be elected!" At Choate, Jack's intelligence and affinity for other students were recognized from the outset—but so were his academic undependability, rebelliousness, love of pranks, and, in the words of then headmaster George St. John, his "tendency to foster a gang spirit." By 1963 the headmastership of Choate had passed from the elder St. John to his son Seymour.

~ *Peggy and Seymour St. John; handwritten note*

Headmaster's Study
November 22nd

Our dear Jackie—and Caroline and John:

Words cannot carry our message; but our hearts share the depth of your grief.

Jack is in loving arms. We are deeply proud of him, and hold him forever a part of us.

Faithfully and devotedly,
Peggy and Seymour St. John

Jack Kennedy entered Harvard College in the fall of 1936, after brief stints at both the London School of Economics and Princeton the previous year. Little more than a year later, Franklin Delano Roosevelt appointed Joseph Kennedy as Ambassador to Great Britain. In 1939 Harvard junior JFK spent the spring semester and following summer touring Europe, the Soviet Union, and the Middle East collecting firsthand information for the senior honors thesis that would eventually become his first published book, *Why England Slept.* Passing in and out of his father's embassy offices in London provided him a ringside seat for the sorry spectacle of Neville Chamberlain's failing appeasement policies.

Without doubt, Harvard was the educational institution most associated with the Kennedy administration. JFK drew heavily from its administration and faculty to staff top positions, completed his term as Harvard overseer even after being elected President, and intended his presidential library to be housed adjacent to its Business School, along the Charles River. Harvard president Nathan Pusey's November telegram and December letter to Mrs. Kennedy talked about "our most illustrious contemporary alumnus" and evoked the "unbreakable link between your husband and his University."

In the early months of 1943, Jack Kennedy and several of his friends from six months of training on the West Coast and at the Navy's boat school in Melville, Rhode Island, shipped out to the Solomon Islands. There, they would become skippers aboard several of the Navy's Patrol Torpedo, or PT, boats. It was no coincidence that many PT boat captains were Ivy Leaguers, since the Navy was looking for good students who had experience handling sailing craft. Late on the night of August 1, 1943, Kennedy's PT boat, *109,* was rammed and capsized by a Japanese destroyer. The unlikely survival of the boat's entire crew—an exploit written up by John Hersey in *The New Yorker* in 1944, and reprinted in condensed form in *Reader's Digest*—helped launch Jack Kennedy's postwar political career.

Beyond politics, the comradely ties formed among veterans of the

South Pacific showed remarkable resilience over the years. President Kennedy brought some of his PT boat companions into the administration—men like James Reed in the Treasury; Paul Fay, Undersecretary of the Navy; and Bill Battle, appointed Ambassador to Australia. At least two of Mrs. Kennedy's correspondents were fellow *PT-109* crew members from Massachusetts. Maurice Kowal from Uxbridge was "regarded by some of his mates as their leading wit," according to Robert J. Donovan, author of *PT 109: John F. Kennedy in WW II.* Wounded in the leg from Japanese airplane fire, Kowal left Kennedy's boat before it was sunk, but showed up again after the legendary rescue to participate in the gunboat activities of *PT-59* that Kennedy later commanded. Charles Harris was a gunner's mate from Watertown, Massachusetts, who was shipwrecked when *PT-109* was rammed; despite a wound in his leg, he, along with the eight other sailors, was able to hang on to a coconut log and swim to temporary refuge on a nearby island. Lt. Kennedy, meanwhile, was using the straps of a life jacket to tug to safety another mate who was too badly burned to hold on to the log.

❧ *Maurice L. Kowal; handwritten letter*

Dec. 6, 1963

Dear Mrs Kennedy:

. . . I will always remember President Kennedy when I knew him so well in the Pacific as these are my most treasured memories of him. . . .

I would gladly and willingly give my life to spare so great a man not in title but as a person.

Sincerely,

Maurice L. Kowal

ɞ *Charles A. Harris; handwritten letter*

Nov. 27, 1963

My dear Mrs. Kennedy,

I know you do not know me personally but I am one of the crew members of your Husbands P.T. 109.

I wanted to send a telegram with my condolences but it seemed too cold & short.

Your husband was one of the greatest men I will ever have the honor to meet. I am only sorry I never had the honor to meet you, his wonderful wife. . . .

In my mind & heart you were married to one of the greatest men in our time & time to come. I don't think he would have hurt a soul intentionally he was that much of a Christian & if the rest of the world could have been the same there would be no more tragedy. . . .

Sincerely & Love to the Children,

Charles A. Harris

One of the moving tales about Kennedy's days in the South Pacific came from a Navy chaplain who struck up a shipboard acquaintance with the lieutenant.

ɞ *Graham Gilmer Jr., M.D.; handwritten and typewritten letters*

Orange, California

January 18, 1964

Dear Mrs. Kennedy,

. . . . It occurred to me that you might possibly appreciate a story from our President's life . . . Therefore I have taken the liberty of sending you a copy of the letter I wrote my parents . . . last November 22.

My dear Father and Mother,

The night is dark—and the darkness seems even deeper in this world. Twenty years ago at about this date, a young naval officer came aboard my ship—*The Breton*—wounded and for transportation back to the states. He boarded at Espiritu Santos in The New Hebrides. As chaplain of the ship I knew that our orders would probably cause us to be underway on Christmas Day. So a few days before we weighed anchor, the doctor and I went ashore and gathered palm fronds to "make a Christmas tree."

In due time the Christmas tree was finished—a marvel of engineering—being made of a wooded pole with holes drilled for the palm fronds. . . . And there on Christmas morn 1943 our ship's personnel and passengers exchanged and opened our meagre gifts before a tree that was probably much more like the trees about Bethlehem that first Christmas morn so long ago. This young naval officer circulated among the more seriously wounded from Bougainville Island, lending cheer and the Christmas Spirit throughout the day. He also was present at the ship's Christmas Party later in the day as we crossed the International Date Line. And for this reason, the next day was Christmas all over again. For this second Christmas we had no special celebration. But who cared? We were heading home from the holocaust of war and in a real sense—every day was Christmas.

Particularly apropos to the Christmas spirit of "Peace on Earth—Good Will unto all Men" was this extra Christmas to the young naval officer of whom I speak. For he had been tried in the cauldron of war and had "quitted himself as a man." And during the days at sea he read extensively from our ship's library—and on the various occasions I talked with him, he spoke of his dream of a peaceful world.

God did not allot to him the consummation of his vision of worldwide peace in his time but He did grant to him an extra Christmas Day in life.

Lt. (jg) John F. Kennedy and the crew of the PT-*109*. Solomon Islands, 1943. Probable identification: Back row: Allan Webb, Leon Drawdy, Edgar Mauer, Edmund Drewitch, John Maguire, Kennedy. Front row: Charles Harris, Maurice Kowal, Andrew Kirksey, Lenny Thom. *JFK Library*

And thus John F. Kennedy lived in his 46 years through 47 Christmases—for it was of him that I was speaking above.

Love,
Graham

Kennedy's wartime heroism sprung also from deep convictions formed during his father's stormy days as ambassador in London. The senior Kennedy was a well-known anti-interventionist whose attitudes held sway with older son Joe longer than with Jack. Nonetheless, Joe Jr. changed his tune quickly when Pearl Harbor was hit. And it was Joe Jr. who lost his life in 1944 when his explosives-laden bomber detonated in midair over Britain. His death ensured that any presidential ambitions ex-Ambassador Kennedy had for his sons would shift onto the younger one.

Jack had developed an early partiality to the British cause partly on account of his younger sister Kathleen, or "Kick." Kathleen was said to have "the soul of an expatriate"; her introduction to British society via the American Embassy in London succeeded so well that she became an ardent Anglophile . . . and a favorite of multiple young English beaux. Among these were William Douglas-Home, who became a well-known playwright; Lord Tony Rosslyn (Anthony St.-Clair Erskine, Earl of Rosslyn); and most of all, William Cavendish, Marquess of Hartington and heir to the Dukedom of Devonshire, with whom Kick fell passionately in love and decided to marry, despite his Protestant upbringing. The union was vehemently opposed by Rose Kennedy, who threatened to disown her daughter for abandoning the faith of her ancestors. Luckily Kick had been adopted by no less a social figure than the American-born heiress Nancy, Viscountess Astor, who acted as go-between for mother and daughter.

When Kick was killed in an airplane accident in the South of France in 1948, the eulogies poured in from all over Great Britain. "No American . . . was ever so loved as she" wrote an anonymous correspondent to the London *Times*. Now, fifteen years later, some of the same people wrote to Jacqueline Kennedy about her slain husband. Wrote William Douglas-Home: "I loved that man. I never knew a nicer, greater man." Nancy, Lady Astor, wired "LOVE AND DEEPEST SYMPATHY TO YOU ALL," while her daughter-in-law Chiquita Astor wrote that Jack "was the one man I admired most through the years. One knew him, one had seen him grow and gain stature to the point that the whole world was focused on him." Moucher Devonshire, mother-in-law of Kick, wired that she was "OVERWHELMED BY TERRIBLE NEWS," while the Earl of Rosslyn, Kathleen Kennedy's onetime admirer, wrote:

~~ *Anthony Rosslyn; handwritten letter*

Petersfield

Hants.

25/11/63

Dear Mrs. Kennedy,

As soon as I heard that dreadful news my thoughts turned to you &
the children, & I sent you that telegram. I am surrounded in this room by
pictures of him & "Kick," & his autographed books are near me too. He
was very much part of my pre-war life & when we met at your sister's for
the christening, we talked of those days. What a senseless, wicked tragedy, & what an appalling shock & ordeal for you, your high courage will

STONERWOOD PARK.
PETERSFIELD.
HANTS.
PETERSFIELD 433.

25/11/63

DEAR MRS. KENNEDY,
AS SOON AS I HEARD THAT
DREADFUL NEWS MY THOUGHTS TURNED TO
YOU & THE CHILDREN, & I SENT YOU
THAT TELEGRAM. I AM SURROUNDED IN
THIS ROOM BY PICTURES OF HIM & "KICK,"
& HIS AUTOGRAPHED BOOKS ARE NEAR ME
TOO. HE WAS VERY MUCH PART OF MY
PRE-WAR LIFE & WHEN WE MET AT
YOUR SISTER'S FOR THE CHRISTENING, WE
TALKED OF THOSE DAYS. WHAT A SENSELESS,
WICKED TRAGEDY & WHAT AN APPALLING
SHOCK & ORDEAL FOR YOU, YOUR HIGH
COURAGE WILL MAKE IT MORE BEARABLE.
YOU ARE SO MUCH IN MY THOUGHTS &
PRAYERS & I HOPE THAT ONE DAY WE MAY
MEET AGAIN. WITH MY LOVE
TONY (ROSSLYN)

make it more bearable. You are so much in my thoughts & prayers & I
hope that one day we may meet again. With my love

Tony (Rosslyn)

By the time the Kennedys began summering in Hyannis Port in 1926
the railroad had turned the town into a popular resort. Jack was ten when
the boys first acquired a sailboat, named the *Rose Elizabeth* after their
mother. Before long he was winning races on his own secondhand Wianno
Senior, the *Victura*. Jack's experiences on the water gave him a lifelong love
for the sea not only as an arena where he could overcome his physical frailty
(as an adolescent and young man, he was constantly in and out of infir-
maries and hospitals), but as a refuge apart from the stress of official cares.
Coincidentally, the ocean also brought the President and a total stranger
together for a moment of natural communion.

২৺ *Michael H—*[*]*; typewritten letter*

26 Jan 64

Dear Mrs. Kennedy:

Let me introduce myself, my name is Michael H———. I am in the Air
Force here at Hickem Field, Hawaii. I am attached with the Medical Sqd.
The job I have is with Military Public Health. . . .

You may be asking yourself why I wrote this so late, well things were
busy for you and you wouldn't have gotten this letter. I still don't know if
you will. . . .

You see I met Mr. Kennedy one day on the beach. You know how he
liked to walk on the beach. Well I was setting on the beach thinking of

---

[*] The author of this letter requested anonymity.

NAVAL AIDE TO THE PRESIDENT

December 3, 1963

Dear Mrs. Kennedy,

I cannot tell you how much I was touched by your kindness and thoughtfulness in sending me the President's lighter. I shall treasure it always.

The greatest privilege of my life will have been to have served the man who I know was God's chosen one to set the course for this stumbling and divided nation. He gave me a new insight into the beauty and basic goodness

From Tazewell Shepard, White House Naval Aide and a favorite of President Kennedy's; in the days after the tragedy, Mrs. Kennedy gave him JFK's cigarette lighter.

of the human spirit — and
of the heights in virtue and
noble purpose that one may
reach if he dedicates his
heart and mind to that end.

I will forever be in
your and his debt. You
will honor me to call me
for anything that I can
ever do for you or your
children — now, or at
any time in the future.

With greatest respect,

Tay

something not really paying any attention and he came up behind me. He asked if he might help so I told him but I never looked up. He gave me the answer I was looking for, then I looked up and realized who he was. I jumped up and he laughed so I said thank you, he said that was all right and asked if there was anything else. I know he wasn't used to little problems. But when he helped me it seemed so wonderful of him for he was such a busy man and to take time for me well I think you understand. . . .

All I can say is I pray for him and you. He was everything they said. . . .

Sincerely,

Michael H——

While Jack Kennedy served in the Navy and began recovering from wartime trauma, his future wife, Jacqueline, was finishing her primary and secondary education—at the Chapin School in Manhattan, Holton-Arms in Washington, D.C., and at Miss Porter's boarding school in Farmington, Connecticut. Necessarily, the letters of sympathy from classmates and school officials to the new widow strike a different note of nostalgia than those remembering the late President.

Loretta A. Flynn, of Southington, Connecticut, was sure that Jacqueline would not remember that she used to shampoo her hair many years earlier when she was a student at Miss Porter's and fondly recalled, "You were a lovely sweet girl thin as you are now but God has given you a lot of strength and courage to weather all your sorrows since then." And Miss Porter's Headmaster, Hollis French, sent a well-turned letter of sympathy "on behalf of the school which you attended and which you have befriended."

Jackie Kennedy had a slightly more complicated relationship with Vassar College, having taken an unofficial junior year abroad in France without requesting formal permission to do so (in the end, Mrs. Kennedy got her college degree from George Washington University in the District of Columbia). Nonetheless, the First Lady cultivated an active relationship with Vassar while in the White House. That sense of connection clearly remained strong, as proven in the following letters from the onetime head of the college's drama club.

Frances Sternhagen, stage and screen actress; handwritten letter

Nov. 23rd, 1963

Dear Jackie,

For the last few years I have felt pleased and quietly proud that I knew you, however slightly, before the world knew you. I drove up to my first Vassar reunion last year with Joan Ferguson Ellis, and we both remarked, on driving home again, that whenever you were mentioned, everyone felt the same way. . . .

But my personal remembrances of you seem to be in only a small way responsible for my feeling. It was, oddly enough, to you as a grown-up woman that I felt the closest—I and a few million other people. . . . You and your husband together represented the best that America had to offer. . . . And perhaps one of the loveliest balances represented by you both was his wonderful sense of humor and your gentleness of heart.

I simply want to add my prayers and heartfelt sympathy to the thousands of others who can do nothing else. . . .

Frances Sternhagen

Other reminiscences bring to life a curious, intellectually engaged national leader and a dedicated, noble, and intensely private wife. Most stand on their own without special commentary. The first is from Josiah Bunting, a young Rhodes Scholar attending Oxford University who would later become a well-known author, college president, and Superintendent of Virginia Military Institute.

ℰ *Josiah Bunting III; typewritten letter*

Christ Church College
Oxford University
10 January

Dear Mrs. Kennedy:

Twice I was privileged to meet our late and beloved president. . . .

In January of 1960, when I was returning in uniform to Virginia Military Institute, I noticed (then) Senator Kennedy sitting across from another cadet and myself in the dining car of a New York–Washington train. He looked over at us and said, "Good morning!" (and then, what floored both of us) "I can tell by your scarlet capes that you are cadets at VMI and not West Point; the red represents the bloodshed of the Corps during the Civil War . . . doesn't it?" We nodded at him, swallowing hard. We were RATS (freshmen) at the time and such knowledge of our little military college from an outsider was incredible. But what made a more ineradicable imprint on my memory was the manner in which this knowledge was offered. Your late husband had a boyish grin on his sunburnt face, and he was clearly enjoying our surprise. . . .

Then, last spring, I was with a contingent of VMI cadets who met President Kennedy briefly in the Rose Garden. I had a painting to present him. . . . He walked out of his office, made right for me, took my hand and said "Mr. Bunting, I heard you won a Rhodes Scholarship and I think that is fine." . . . His knowledge of history was astounding to us, but, again, not as amazing as the fact that he could usually (when introduced to the cadets) remember something about each. . . .

You have probably heard about this . . . final tribute I mention . . .

less than two hours after the awful news reached Oxford, one of the colleges was holding a memorial service attended by students from forty nations. . . .

Yours very sincerely,
Josiah Bunting III
Lieutenant, U.S. Army

John Armstrong; handwritten letter

Colonial Inn
Concord, Massachusetts

Dear Mrs. Kennedy—

I should have written you sooner.

I knew your husband in prep school (Choate) and later on the Cape where we played touch football together. As a matter of fact, I used to take "Kick" out and knew most of the family. One of my most treasured possessions is the book, "As We Remember Joe."

. . . I was brought up the same way as your husband—as an aristocrat with high ambitions, a desire to excel and a deep and abiding admiration for the finer things of life. . . .

Where does the aristocrat, the romantic, the lover of fine things fit into the American world of today? I am very discouraged by what I see all around me. This is not the country it once was.

While I was not a whole-hearted supporter of your husband (too conservative for that), I did admire his pursuit of excellence, his nobility, and, above all, his wit and grace. . . .

Yours sincerely,
John Armstrong

꩜ *Sampson P. Bowers; handwritten letter*

November 26th
Monday

My dear Mrs. Kennedy,

. . . Some of us knew the pleasure of meeting your late husband . . . years ago. He was a junior Senator, I believe, and he and I were flying down to Hobe Sound for a long weekend. . . . He and I had sat together on the plane and talked most of the way. I remember that Senator Saltonstall was aboard and seeing him I remarked that I had always had a great deal of respect for his Yankee determination and his old-fashioned ideas. The Senator said he agreed with me in part but that he was very impatient with the "old school" . . . people . . . dragging their feet.

I reacted very quickly to this and said that I thought "the old school" was the most important thing in the world, because without it there could be no "new school" and he and I would not then be so impatient to be on with it. He got very serious and said that he had never really thought of it that way. . . .

. . . Strangely enough . . . a year or so later I passed him one day in the Washington airport and he called to me to tell me that my remark about the "old school" and the "new school" had profoundly affected his outlook toward the role that history played in the development of a new idea. That he was forever grateful to me for my contribution to his personal philosophy.

That's the way my life was touched by this great man. . . .

Most respectfully,
Sampson P. Bowers

Jack Kennedy's history of ailments dated back to his having scarlet fever as a child. The following letter is only one of several from various of his doctors, who all regarded him highly.

VICTOR F. MARSHALL, M. D.
525 EAST 68TH STREET
NEW YORK 21, N. Y.

TRAFALGAR 9-9000

November 25, 1963.

Dear Mrs. Kennedy,

You may recall that I am the urologist from the New York Hospital who has seen your husband a number of times since 1955 with Doctors Travell and Burkley.

No words of mine can convey my full sympathy to you and your family. In addition to his superb qualities as one of our greatest Presidents, he was a real man. I never had a better patient. In spite of his deservedly high position, conversations could be direct and clear. He could grasp medical connotations with amazing ease, yet this was not his field. I am proud to have had the honor, and pleasure, of knowing him in something less than a purely formal way. If ever I can be of help, I shall be only too glad.

Most sincerely,

Victor Marshall

✍ Dr. Victor F. Marshall; handwritten letter

Victor F. Marshall, M.D.
New York, NY
November 25, 1963

Dear Mrs. Kennedy,

You may recall that I am the urologist from the New York Hospital who has seen your husband a number of times since 1955 with Doctors Travell and Burkley.

No words of mine can convey my full sympathy to you and your family. In addition to his superb qualities as one of our greatest Presidents, he was a real man. I never had a better patient. . . . He could grasp medical connotations with amazing ease, yet this was not his field. I am proud to have had the honor, and pleasure, of knowing him in something less than a purely formal way. . . .

Most sincerely,
Victor Marshall

The last three letters in this chapter all come from members of a single family who were frequent guests at the White House and at Camp David—Paul and Anita Fay and their daughter.

🖝 *Paul "Red" Fay, Undersecretary of the Navy, JFK PT boat pal, and close friend; handwritten letter*

The Under Secretary of the Navy
Washington
5 Dec 63

My dearest Jacqueline,

Going through a Navy shipyard in Seattle I received the stunning report that "The Chief" was dead. Since that awful moment I have tried in vain to put on paper the love and sorrow that I hold for you. It is impossible to put the excitement, the joy, the friendship of a lifetime on a few pages. . . . Never before have I realized the finality of death. . . . But this at least I know: you had the love and I shared the friendship of the only man in my short span of years who was touched with greatness. . . .

Somewhere in wherever is Heaven and possibly it is unseen and untouchable right around us, I like believing that Jack is silently and unseen watching with pride his "Buttons," "You rascal John John," but most his proud beautiful wife who by her example has made all us Americans a little taller and so proud.

For now and always
in "your corner"
Red

🖝 *Anita Fay; handwritten letter*

Dearest Jackie,

From the minute I met the President I was like an excited child on the night before Christmas. . . . From the beginning of Red's and my life together the most exciting thing that could happen to us would be a telephone call from Jack Kennedy. . . . Now knowing the phone will never ring again we are heartbroken and knowing our sorrow we die inside for you.

Love,
Anita

&c *Katherine F. Fay; handwritten letter*

McLean, Virginia

Dear Jackie,

I will never forget when I first met the President. I was sitting on his lap in San Francisco and he was telling me about when he would become President, he'd invite me over to the White House. Even at that early date, I knew it would come true. It certainly came true, but it all went too quickly. I still to this day don't wholly believe what happened. The President to me has always been my dream man. Every time I saw him I thought my heart would never calm down. When daddy told me to kiss him goodnight at Camp David I shied away with embarrassment. Now I wish I could have kissed and hugged him a million times. . . .

I will pray for you
Sincerely yours
Katherine F. Fay

Four

POLITICAL FRIENDS AND FOES

When Air Force One landed at Andrews Air Force Base in the early evening hours of November 22, Lyndon Johnson waited on board until the ambulance bearing JFK's coffin had driven away. Emerging with his wife, Lady Bird, at his side, he spoke to the American people:

> *This is a sad time for all people. We have suffered a loss that cannot be weighed. For me it is a deep personal tragedy. I know the world shares the sorrow that Mrs. Kennedy and her family bear. I will do my best. That is all I can do. I ask for your help—and God's.*

The new President went straight from Andrews Air Force Base to the White House, his helicopter landing in the same spot from where the Kennedys had taken off the previous morning. He walked to his office in the beaux arts bulk of the Executive Office Building across the street from the West Wing of the White House. After making calls to former Presidents Truman and Eisenhower and FBI Director J. Edgar Hoover, Johnson sat at his desk and scribbled perhaps the first two of the deluge of condolence letters that would flood the White House in the coming weeks. The first note was to John F. Kennedy Jr.

‌*President Lyndon B. Johnson to John Fitzgerald Kennedy Jr.; handwritten note*

November 22, 1963
7:20 Friday Night

Dear John—

It will be many years before you fully understand what a great man your father was. His loss is a deep personal tragedy for all of us, but I wanted you particularly to know that I share your grief—You can always be proud of him—

Affectionately,
Lyndon B. Johnson

‌*President Lyndon B. Johnson to Caroline Kennedy; handwritten note*

Friday night 7:30
November 22, 1963

Dearest Caroline—

Your father's death has been a great tragedy for the nation, as well as for you, and I wanted you to know how much my thoughts are with you at this time.

He was a wise and devoted man. You can always be proud of what he did for his country—

Affectionately,
Lyndon B. Johnson

The tensions and mistrust that had always divided the close political friends of John and Robert Kennedy from the Vice President reemerged quickly in the chaos triggered by the assassination. Wounds festered from the fight for the 1960 nomination and immediately after: when JFK won, he had offered Johnson the Vice Presidential spot; then, once Johnson accepted, he sent Bobby to try to convince him to change his mind. Resentment toward the new President was not confined to family and political aides. It also quickly flared among partisans at the grassroots level, as attested to by this letter from William Liebenow, a former PT boat mate of the dead President whose letter of concern to President Johnson ended up among the condolence letters to Mrs. Kennedy.

ᘒ *William F. Liebenow to President Lyndon B. Johnson; handwritten letter*

Nov. 27, 1963

Dear Mr. President,

Last night I attended a meeting of the Kent County Citizens for Kennedy-Johnson. The meeting opened with tributes to our late President and high sounding phrases uttered about carrying on his work.

It was suggested that the name of the group be changed to Citizens for Kennedy Ideals or some more appropriate name. From then on, Mr. President, the meeting deteriorated into a political brawl of name calling and accusations. On one side the members of the State Democratic Central Committee were lined up against the original members of the old Citizens for Kennedy group. I am rather naive about politics, but finally got the floor and asked for a direct yes or no answer, as to whether the State Central Committee was against President Johnson.

Somebody yelled out, "Now you're wising up." That's all the answer I got.

Mr. President there is something wrong with the Democratic Party in Michigan.

I was boat captain of the PT 157 that picked up Kennedy and his crew after their ordeal in the Pacific. Though always a Democrat, Kennedy gave me a personal interest in politics. In his memory and for the good of the party the old scars of 1960 must be forever healed.

Mr. President it sure looks like we need help!

Sincerely,
William F. Liebenow
Alto, Michigan

It's not surprising that the New Frontiersmen of the Kennedy presidency had trouble adjusting to LBJ as their new president. Johnson was viewed

Vice President Lyndon Johnson and President Kennedy, in the Oval Office, September 17, 1963. *Abbie Rowe, White House/JFK Library*

as the epitome of the small-time politico, while JFK had been seen as transcending the world of common politicians and government officials. Those taken into Kennedy's circle seemed to belong to an almost new species of political creature. They were seen as more vital, more refined, oriented to the future, ready to break out of the materialistic striving and "cultural mediocrity" of the 1950s. With a few rifle shots in Dallas, it seemed to many that the country had been plunged back into the vulgar world of corrupt backroom deals.

The loyalty Kennedy inspired was intense and personal. In a Friday note to Jackie, special assistant Arthur Schlesinger called working for him "the most fulfilling experience I have ever had or could imagine." From those with personal connections, this could be expected. According to his wife, Bonny, William Battle, the U.S. Ambassador to Australia and former South Pacifc U.S. Navy veteran, "would have done anything . . . or gone anywhere" the President asked. Kennedy's charisma also had a strong effect on most everyone brought into JFK's circle. Assistant Secretary of State Phillips Talbot expressed the depth of many New Frontiersmen's devotion when he wrote the First Lady, "Let me say frankly that I accepted the invitation to come to Washington because I believed that your husband expressed our hope for America and the world. . . . I believed in him fervently."

❧ *James Braxton Craven Jr., United States District Judge; telegram*

MORGANTOWN NC NOV 25 12:44 PM
MRS JOHN F KENNEDY HYANNIS PORT MASS
I WOULD RATHER HAVE BEEN APPOINTED A FEDERAL
JUDGE BY YOUR LATE HUSBAND THAN BY ANY OF THE
OTHER GREAT PRESIDENTS OF HISTORY BECAUSE HE SYM-
BOLIZED ALL THE BEST OF MY GENERATION COME TO
POWER. . . . OUR DEEPEST . . . SYMPATHY AND ADMIRATION
JAMES BRAXTON CRAVEN JR

❧ *David C. Acheson, United States Attorney for the District of Columbia;*
handwritten letter

Nov. 25, 1963

My dear Mrs. Kennedy—

While it cannot diminish your own tragic loss, perhaps it is a comfort
to you to see such massive evidence of the appreciation in which the late
President was held by the country. I think his administration was a great
one meaning it closely reflected him. He had, I think, a unique sense of
the greatness and historic worth—and potential—of his office, and this
sense together with his own qualities gave our public life an elevated standard which has left our country better than it was. I was and am proud to
have been associated with him. . . .

My most profound sympathy and deep respect.

David C. Acheson

Washington politicians had never been quite sure what to make of Jacqueline Kennedy, although once her CBS television special tour of the
White House captivated a national audience, they recognized her allure
for the public. The regal composure she displayed in the days immediately
following Dallas astounded even the converted. James Symington was an
aide to Bobby Kennedy in the Justice Department. He and his wife, Sylvia,
offered Jackie this succinct but elegant tribute: "We were bound to share
your grief. Now we would be proud and grateful to share your courage."
Many other voices joined the chorus of praise. Edmund Muskie, later the
ill-fated early front-runner candidate for the 1972 presidential nomination,
was quick to perceive the calming, exemplary nature of her behavior.

❧ *Edmund Muskie, U.S. Senator from Maine; handwritten letter*

> United States Senate
> Washington D.C.

Dear Mrs. Kennedy,

There is no way—and I am sure you would not take it if there were—to lift the burden of grief which you bear.

There is a way, which you have found and so valiantly displayed, to make your grief serve the country which you have both served and loved so well.

The President surely has watched over you and blessed you these past four days as you have walked with such clear prayers and firm steps, leading the rest of us in our grief, showing us the way to honor his memory. . . .

> Sincerely yours,
> Ed

The dedication Jackie manifested for both husband and children earned her tributes from other political families.

❧ *Lindy Boggs, wife of Hale Boggs, Louisiana Congressman and Majority Whip, U.S. House of Representatives; handwritten letter*

Dear Jackie,

Just now I have returned from mass. This is the only definite way I know to help you. Somehow these past few days I have felt that the prayers of an entire nation have flowed through your every graceful motion.

. . . The example of your heroic womanhood and your gentle but firm motherhood is the most beautiful face America has ever presented to the rest of the world. . . .

Sincerely,

Lindy Boggs

ॐ *Betty Fulbright, wife of J. William Fulbright, U.S. Senator from Arkansas; handwritten letter*

Monday

Dear Jackie-

It is *still* unbelievable—

He was so exactly what I had always hoped a President of our country would one day be—

I know there is little solace to be had at such a moment as this;—but in time, it cannot *but* be a comfort to you,—the knowledge that you were so exactly the right First Lady to such a President. . . .

Betty Fulbright

One of the great charms the Kennedys held for the public was the "First Family" image conveyed by photographs of the President with Caroline or John-John playing under his desk or romping in the Oval Office. Not since Frances Cleveland had there been such a young First Lady, and not since Teddy Roosevelt had there been young children living full-time in the White House. At the same time, Jackie did her utmost to provide a normal, protected environment for her two children.

Orville Freeman, Secretary of Agriculture, and his wife and children; hand-written card accompanying potted plant

My dear Mrs. Kennedy,

. . . We have become great admirers of you and your husband. Perhaps one of the things we have admired most was the gentle, understanding way in which both of you have helped your children. . . .

This plant was developed at the Agricultural Experimental Station at Beltsville, Md. In the spring perhaps you and the children would enjoy a visit there to see other plants and the many baby pigs, lambs, calves, etc. We would be happy to assist you to make the visit a strictly private one.

Orv, Jane, Connie, and Mike Freeman

Kennedy's initial attempts to deal with his Communist adversaries were met with setbacks. He struggled to escape the straitjacket of Cold War politics with little success, although with the help of close allies like Defense Secretary Robert McNamara and his brother Bobby he was able to fend off the cataclysmic confrontations urged on him from his first days in office. His long-standing skepticism about the wisdom of senior military officers was confirmed by the bad intelligence and bungled planning for the Bay of Pigs invasion. But he felt he was too weak politically to attempt a complete makeover of the defense establishment. Among those military officers who sent condolence telegrams to his widow were Curtis LeMay and Chairman of the Joint Chiefs Lyman Lemnitzer. Both were holdovers, and neither showed much interest in implementing Kennedy's and Defense Secretary McNamara's new military doctrine of "flexible response."

੩੭ *General Lyman Lemnitzer, former chairman, Joint Chiefs of Staff; telegram*

FM SACEUR
TO: MRS JOHN F. KENNEDY
NATO UNCLASSIFIED

BOTH PERSONALLY AND [ON] BEHALF OF ALL MEM-
BERS OF THE MILITARY COMMUNITY OF ALLIED COM-
MAND EUROPE, I EXTEND TO YOU AND YOUR FAMILY
OUR HEARTFELT CONDOLENCES IN YOUR TRAGIC
LOSS.

OUR SENSE OF BEREAVEMENT IS ESPECIALLY KEEN
BECAUSE OF THE SUPPORT WHICH PRESIDENT KEN-
NEDY, AS A GREAT STATESMAN, TIRELESSLY GAVE TO
THE NORTH ATLANTIC ALLIANCE, AND THE UNDER-
STANDING WHICH, AS A FORMER MEMBER OF THE
UNITED STATES ARMED FORCES, HE HAD FOR THE AS-
PIRATIONS AND INTERESTS WHICH MOST DIRECTLY
CONCERN MILITARY MEN AND THEIR FAMILIES. . . .

L. L. LEMNITZER
GENERAL, U.S. ARMY
SUPREME ALLIED COMMANDER, EUROPE

Curtis LeMay was often lampooned for his advocacy of total war (and
even caricatured as Jack D. Ripper in the 1964 movie *Dr. Strangelove or:
How I Learned to Stop Worrying and Love the Bomb*).

📚 *General Curtis LeMay, U.S. Air Force Chief of Staff, future running mate of presidential candidate George Wallace; typewritten letter*

Washington

November 22, 1963

Dear Mrs. Kennedy:

On behalf of the men and women of the United States Air Force, may I extend our deepest sympathy for the tragic loss of your husband.

His strength has been the nation's strength. His loss is the Free World's loss. The marks he has left behind will serve as a monument and inspiration to us all.

Sincerely,

Curtis E. LeMay

John Kennedy was able to capture the allegiance of most of America's laboring class like no president since FDR, and the heads of most unions knew it. Labor leaders like the United Auto Workers' Walter Reuther played a key role in bringing along white support for civil rights, while the more conservative George Meany, president of the AFL-CIO, appreciated Kennedy's willingness to publicly chastise the executives of the U.S. steel industry until they rescinded what Kennedy considered unconscionable price increases. Meany sent a telegram praising America's lost leader as "the warm friend of all the working people of America." On the day after the funeral, his union issued an official, many-paged eulogy in elaborate calligraphy; its recitation of JFK's accomplishments led off with praise of his important role in increasing the minimum wage. From the left side of the organized labor spectrum, International Longshoremen's union leader Harry Bridges sent his "regrets and sympathy" despite failing to see "eye to eye on many political matters."

John Fitzgerald Kennedy was never as liberal as many of his most vocal supporters wished, whatever the promise of his often forward-looking assertions. When he died from an assassin's bullet, progressives often ascribed to him many of their own values, perhaps out of fear that the liberal promise of the Kennedy era would remain unfulfilled. Back in October 1960 James McGregor Burns had predicted that should Kennedy die in a plane crash, he would be seen universally as a "liberal martyr." And so was he hailed—for good reason and bad—in many of the eulogies, memorial services, and correspondence of the day.

One Kennedy adviser who played a key role in setting the administration's basically liberal agenda toward labor and the economy was Arthur Goldberg, his Secretary of Labor.

❧ *Arthur Goldberg, Supreme Court Justice, former Secretary of Labor; handwritten note*

November 28, 1963

Dear Jackie

You lived the prayer and we saw clearly the meaningfulness of that other prayer: "Lord, make of me an instrument of thy peace . . . that I may not seek to be consoled so much as to console . . ."

And you did that. You consoled and we must thank you for that. May you continue to find strength that sustains.

Sincerely,
Arthur and Dorothy

Arthur Goldberg had moved from the Labor Department to become Supreme Court Justice in October of 1962, but left the court when he was persuaded by President Johnson to become Ambassador to the UN. Meanwhile the court's most renowned and long-serving icon of liberalism, William O. Douglas, sent Mrs. Kennedy the following note:

᷿ *William O. Douglas, Supreme Court justice; handwritten note*

Washington, D.C.

Nov. 23, 1963

Dear Jackie

My heart is so heavy that words fail me. A sadness has come over the earth
that it never knew. We share your grief: and I wanted you to know that I
am close to you in this dark and lonely hour.

Yours faithfully

(W O) Douglas

From Byron "Whizzer" White, the first of Kennedy's appointees to the Supreme Court;
unlike Arthur Goldberg, he served out one of the longest Supreme Court terms of the
twentieth century.

Once the world had survived the Cuban Missile Crisis with a clear Russian setback, Kennedy felt he could afford a more cooperative attitude toward the Soviet Union, at least on the question of nuclear war. In his noted "Peace Speech" at American University on June 10, 1963, he relied partially on suggestions drafted by Norman Cousins, journalist and chairman of the peace organization SANE. Weeks later the United States, United Kingdom, and Soviet Union signed the world's first nuclear test ban treaty in Moscow, signaling a new era of non-nuclear competition between the superpowers. This willingness to curb nuclear weapons, along with the President's switch from a pragmatic political position to a moral position on civil rights, brought him great credit among liberals.

❧ *Dr. Benjamin Spock, pediatrician, bestselling author, and political activist with SANE; handwritten letter*

Cleveland Heights Ohio

Dear Mrs. Kennedy

I have admired your husband for many qualities but most of all for his dignity. For the clarity of his vision and for his courage in fighting for the rights of Negroes and for peace.

I believe that the sacrifices of his death will inspire people with his ideas for generations to come and will further the causes he fought for.

Sincerely,
Benjamin Spock

Dear Mrs Kennedy

I have admired your husband for many qualities but most of all for his dignity. For the clarity of his vision and for his courage in fighting for the rights of Negroes and for peace.

I believe that the sacrifice of his death will inspire people with his ideas for generations to come and will further the causes he fought for.

Sincerely

Benjamin Spock

🙢 *Norman Thomas, six-time presidential candidate of the Socialist Party of America; telegram*

NEW YORK NY 22 447P EST

MRS JOHN F KENNEDY

I CANNOT ADEQUATELY EXPRESS MY DEEP SYMPATHY

FOR YOU AND YOUR FAMILY OR MY SORROW AT THE
SHAMEFUL ASSASSINATION OF YOUR HUSBAND. HE
LIKE LINCOLN WAS A MARTYR TO A DEFENSE OF
EQUALITY OF RIGHT FOR MEN OF ALL COLORS. IT IS
OUR COUNTRY'S SHAME THAT THIS MURDER GREW
OUT OF SUCH WIDELY DISTRIBUTED HATE FOR DE-
CENCY IN HUMAN RELATIONS.

NORMAN THOMAS

In the early stages of the 1960 presidential campaign Kennedy's Roman
Catholicism had loomed as a potentially decisive issue—particularly among
some Protestant ministers. In fact, concern over "Popish" influences had
nearly led both Billy Graham and the Reverend Martin Luther King Sr. to
endorse Richard Nixon.

❧ *Rev. Billy Graham, radio and television evangelist; telegram*

MONTREAT NORTH CAROLINA 22 517P EST
MRS JOHN F KENNEDY
THE PRESIDENT'S DEATH IS A NATIONAL TRAGEDY. HE
WAS MY PERSONAL FRIEND AND I FEEL A PERSONAL
LOSS. I AM PRAYING THAT GOD'S STRENGTH AND
COURAGE WILL BE GIVEN TO YOU DURING THIS PE-
RIOD OF SHOCK AND GREAT LOSS. GOD BLESS YOU

BILLY GRAHAM

One of the biggest obstructionists impeding Kennedy's 1963 Civil Rights
Bill was Strom Thurmond, the "Dixiecrat" former Governor and presidential candidate renowned for his strict segregationist views.

๛ *Strom Thurmond, U. S. Senator from South Carolina; telegram*

WASHINGTON DC NOV 22 331P EST
MRS JOHN F KENNEDY
I AM DEEPLY SHOCKED AND REPULSED BY THIS TRAGIC
EVENT. THIS IS INDEED A DAY OF SADNESS FOR OUR
COUNTRY AND I KNOW THAT ALL AMERICANS WILL
MOURN THE PRESIDENTS DEATH. MY PRAYERS ARE
WITH YOU AND YOUR FAMILY. REGARDS
    STROM THURMOND

President Kennedy's policy toward Cuba was laced with so many contradictions it has sometimes been called schizophrenic. On December 29, 1962, at the Orange Bowl in Miami, Florida, JFK celebrated the just-completed return to Florida of members of Brigade 2506 who had been captured by Castro's government during the Bay of Pigs invasion and whose release the Kennedys had just succeeded in negotiating. In November he had told Nikita Khrushchev that the Soviet Premier need not fear a further United States assault "while matters take their present favorable course." When presented with the Brigade's flag at the Orange Bowl, however, he declared, "I can assure you that this flag will be returned to this brigade in a free Havana." In his post-assassination telegram the Brigade's political leader, Manuel Artime, recalled JFK's declaration: "SOME DAY WE HOPE THAT YOU WILL RETURN TO US IN A FREE CUBA." At the time, Artime was running a naval training camp for Cuban exiles in Nicaragua under U.S. sponsorship, ostensibly preparing for a second Bay of Pigs (whatever plans existed were cancelled by Lyndon Johnson).

2. *Carlos Prio Socarrás, former president of Cuba, deposed by Fulgencio Batista in 1952; telegram*

MIAMI BEACH FLO 23
MRS JACQUELINE KENNEDY
TOGETHER WITH MY OWN PERSONAL SYMPATHY PLEASE AC-
CEPT THIS EXPRESSION OF THE PROFOUND SORROW OVER
THE INFAMOUS MURDER OF YOUR HUSBAND WHICH FILLS
THE CUBAN EXILE PEOPLE. THE LATE PRESIDENT AND YOUR-
SELF WARMED THE HEARTS OF ALL OF US CUBANS DURING
PAST YEARS AND NOW YOU CAN BE CERTAIN THAT IN EACH
OF THOSE HEARTS STANDS AN ALTAR TO THE UNFORGET-
TABLE FRIEND OF OUR SUFFERING COUNTRY
CARLOS PRIO SOCARRAS

Given the ambitions of both LBJ and Bobby Kennedy, many Democrats sensed implicitly that in the upcoming 1964 presidential race, anything less than a ticket joining the two men might rip the party apart. Bob Anthony, a former vocalist with the Tommy Dorsey and Eddy Duchin bands who organized a group called Volunteers for Robert F. Kennedy for Vice-President, made this the centerpiece of his May 1964 condolence letter to Jacqueline Kennedy: "Please, help our #1 boy Attorney General Robert F. Kennedy . . . to become Vice-President!!" Johnson, however, picked Hubert Humphrey for his running mate, and Bobby ran for the U.S. Senate from New York and won.

As fate would have it, neither Bobby nor LBJ would be a candidate in the next presidential cycle. Johnson's escalation of the war in Vietnam provoked a full-scale grassroots revolt by many Democrats against the President, further exacerbated by the murder of Martin Luther King Jr.

After Johnson decided not to run and Robert Kennedy was assassinated, supporters of three remaining Democratic candidates for President— Eugene McCarthy, Hubert Humphrey, and George McGovern—battled fiercely among themselves at the unruly 1968 Democratic Convention. In his condolence letter in late 1963, Hubert Humphrey told Jacqueline Kennedy that, to him and his wife, she and her children would "always be America's first family." For his part, George McGovern declared that "President Kennedy was the greatest human being I have known." The

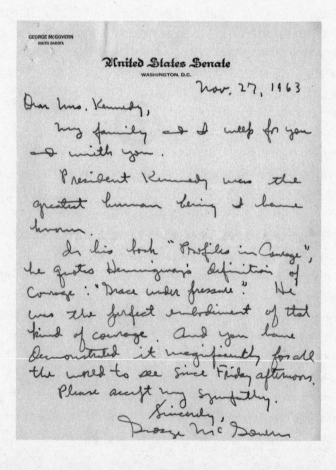

man who would benefit from the ruptured state of the Democratic Party was none other than the man Kennedy had narrowly defeated for president in 1960, Richard Nixon.

> ❧ *Richard Nixon, partner at the legal firm of Nixon, Mudge, Rose, Guthrie & Alexander; recently defeated Republican candidate for Governor of California; letter*

Dear Jackie,

In this tragic hour, Pat and I want you to know that our thoughts and prayers are with you.

While the hand of fate made Jack and me political opponents I always cherish the fact that we were personal friends from the time we came to the Congress together in 1947. That friendship evidenced itself in many ways including the invitation we received to attend your wedding.

Nothing I could say now could add to the splendid tributes which have come from throughout the world.

But I want you to know that the nation will also be forever grateful for your service as First Lady. You brought to the White House charm, beauty and elegance as the official hostess of America, and the mystique of the young in heart which was uniquely yours made an indelible impression on the American consciousness.

If in the days ahead we could be helpful in any way we shall be honored to be at your command.

Sincerely,
Dick Nixon

Throughout America in the early sixties, strong pressures were building from below, on both left and right, culturally and politically. American blacks, emboldened by formal but merely nominal progress on the Federal level, began to press for their full civil rights in some of the most segregated counties in the Deep South. A strong civil rights plank in the 1960 Democratic Party platform and JFK's repeated assurances of his commitment to improving voting rights and access to public accommodations for African-Americans further raised expectations. Kennedy found it galling to see his special rapport with leaders of the African nations endangered by the spectacle of black oppression on his home turf.

The folk culture movement, which had flourished in left-wing circles in the 1930s, was also staging a dramatic comeback. A new wave of young folksingers that included Phil Ochs, Joan Baez, Bob Dylan, and the African-American Odetta was bringing original folk music onto the pop charts (the last three sang at the August 1963 civil rights march on Washington), while black rhythm and blues music began to appeal to young white people under a new term, "soul music." Student activism was also on the rise, animated largely by admiration for the positive press coverage garnered by protesting black students in such movements as SNCC (Student Nonviolent Coordinating Committee).

Programs like the Peace Corps offered an official outlet for youthful idealists anxious to get a taste of the emerging "Third World."

⁊❧ *Frank Mankiewicz, Latin American regional director for the Peace Corps; typewritten note*

November 25

Dear Mrs. Kennedy,

Those of us in the Peace Corps, I think, felt closer to the President than others who did not know him. His vision was our vision, and his spirit and courage and probing mind served as a guide to us all. . . .

Sincerely,
Frank Mankiewicz

Whatever Kennedy's sympathies for civil rights protesters, tensions were inevitable between grassroots activists and leaders in Washington forced to work with Southern elected officials. Freedom Rides to Montgomery, Alabama, in the spring of 1961 brought on white mob violence. Robert Kennedy, who felt the timing of the last protesting bus riders undercut his brother on the eve of his critical summit with Russian leader Khrushchev in Vienna, condemned them. In early October 1962, the enrollment of James Meredith at the University of Mississippi, in Oxford, unleashed a bloody confrontation that could be controlled only with federal forces.

Disagreements within the civil rights movement were also strong, with established organizations like the NAACP focusing more on voting rights while black student groups and King's Southern Christian Leadership Conference (SCLC) pressed for the opening up of public accommodations. A similar conflict had existed between black educator Booker T. Washington and more aggressive black leaders since at least the turn of the century. One of the more salient of the telegrams to arrive in Mrs. Kennedy's condolence mail came from Washington's eighty-something daughter, Portia Washington Pittman, who sent "deepest sympathy."

A more crafty way of negotiating the divide between civil rights activists and the white establishment was represented by Harlem's Adam Clayton Powell. A shrewd operator, Powell burnished his militant credentials while simultaneously concluding mutually beneficial political compacts with white candidates like Dwight Eisenhower, Lyndon Johnson, and John Kennedy.

🙚 *Adam Clayton Powell, African-American pastor and politician and influential U.S. Congressman from Harlem; telegram*

MRS. JOHN F. KENNEDY
THE WHITE HOUSE
WORDS FAIL ME. HE WAS A MARTYR FOR FREEDOM AND
FOR HUMAN RIGHTS. ALL MY PRAYERS. SINCERELY
ADAM C. POWELL

Martin Luther King Jr.'s spring 1963 mobilization in Birmingham, Alabama, led to infamous pictures of Southern police using water hoses and attack dogs on children and youths. Attacks on African-American churches, homes, and hotels, in turn, set off the first black urban riot of the 1960s. One of the more obscurely significant letters to Mrs. Kennedy came from a lawyer named Charles Nice, the sole Alabama representative to dissent from his fellow white legislators when they condemned the Supreme Court for banning segregation in schools. Nice had also been a behind-the-scenes voice for reason during the Birmingham unrest.

🙚 *Charles M. Nice, attorney and former Alabama legislator; typewritten letter*

Birmingham, Alabama
November 26th, 1963

Dear Mrs. Kennedy:

   I want to express my deepest sympathy over your tremendous loss. I also feel like I have suffered a great personal tragedy.

   Never has a President made such an impact on the world in such a short time.

All the world admired the magnificent way you bore yourself during these past three days. What great inner strength you have; how proud your husband would be of you.

Now he, too, belongs to the ages. With deepest sympathy, I am

Sincerely yours,

Charles M. Nice, Jr.

In the wake of the troubles in Birmingham and a showdown with Alabama Governor George Wallace on June 11, President Kennedy decided on the spur of the moment, that same day, to deliver a major televised address explaining to the nation why he was finally introducing major civil rights legislation. The speech became one of the key moments defining his political legacy. In it, he called passage of the bill a "moral issue" that could wait no longer.

That same night after midnight, some ninety miles south of Greenville, Mississippi, the African-American director of that state's NAACP, Medgar Evers, was ambushed and killed by a deer rifle as he approached the front door of his home.

ᔐ *Myrlie (Mrs. Medgar) Evers, widow of slain NAACP civil rights leader; telegram*

JACKSON MISS
I EXTEND TO YOU AND YOUR FAMILY MY SINCEREST CONDOLENCE ON THE TRAGIC DEATH OF YOUR HUSBAND. I KNOW WORDS CAN BE OF LITTLE COMFORT NOW FOR I LOST MY HUSBAND ON JUNE 12TH IN THE SAME WAY. THE ENTIRE WORLD SHARES YOUR GREAT LOSS AND SORROW.
MRS. MEDGAR EVERS

Attorney General Robert Kennedy and Vice President Johnson with Martin Luther King Jr. (left) and Roy Wilkins after meeting at the White House with President Kennedy and other civil rights leaders, June 22, 1963. *Abbie Rowe, White House/JFK Library*

The lives and careers of Martin Luther King and John Fitzgerald Kennedy had been crucially intertwined ever since JFK's October 1960 call to Martin Luther King's wife while the preacher was in a Georgia state prison. The relationship between the living men, however, was never a comfortable one. Harris Wofford had played a critical role as the President's campaign liaison with King and his SCLC. After Wofford was passed over for a Justice Department position because he was considered too close to King and others, he served for sixteen months as the White House liaison to civil rights groups before becoming the Peace Corps special representative to Africa and heading up the rapid buildup of the Peace Corps in Ethiopia. Thus Wofford, who more than any Kennedy aide brought about the connection between Martin Luther King and the Kennedys, was out of the country during the crucial turning point of the civil rights struggle in 1963. In his letter to Jacqueline Kennedy from Addis Ababa, Wofford spoke of "the admiration and respect—the devotion—I had for your husband," and evoked the "sunny afternoon, on the eve of the election," when Kennedy, "holding Caroline by the hand . . . walked toward his campaign plane, and I sensed he was walking into history." Before he departed that day, Kennedy gave Wofford his personal assurance that, although he would not sign then the report on constitutional rights Wofford had brought for that purpose—which called for strong and immediate civil rights legislation—he would do so once elected. Marooned outside Addis Ababa, Ethiopia, on November 22, Wofford made a mad dash for the airport with the idea of talking his way onto the field to go aboard Haile Selassie's plane, but arrived just as the jet was lifting off for D.C. and the funeral.

At the end of August 1963 came the massive march on Washington at which Martin Luther King delivered his "I have a dream" speech; two weeks later four young Negro girls were killed in the basement of the Sixteenth Street Baptist Church in Birmingham when a huge bomb exploded there. To the disappointment of activists, Kennedy, instead of sending federal peacekeepers, sent a pair of emissaries to "study" the situation in the city and calm nerves on all sides. King was disappointed, but remained convinced that with his June 11 speech Kennedy had indeed finally understood the deeper significance of the civil rights movement. In his oral history at the JFK Library, King accused the Kennedy administration of "crystallizing tokenism" during its first two years. But then, said King, Kennedy "went through what Lincoln went through . . . over this question of signing the Emancipation Proclamation. He vacillated a good deal. . . . Finally, the events caused him to see that he had to do this, and he came to the moral conclusion that he had to do it no matter what it meant." When he heard at home in Atlanta that Kennedy had been slain, King said to his wife, Coretta: "This is what is going to happen to me also." She had no answer. Three days later he was at the Washington funeral as a bystander, without a formal invitation from anyone at the White House.

ᔓ *Rev. and Mrs. Martin Luther King Sr. and Dr. and Mrs. Martin Luther King Jr., civil rights leaders; telegram*

ATLANTA GA 24 225P EST
MRS JOHN F KENNEDY
MAY GOD GIVE YOU AND YOUR FAMILY THE STRENGTH AND COURAGE YOU NEED IN THIS HOUR OF BEREAVE-MENT WE PRAY THAT YOU MAY TAKE COURAGE IN THE FACT THAT YOU KNEW A GREAT MAN SO INTIMATELY A MAN WHO THOUGH YOUNG IN YEARS AND WHO SERVED HIS COUNTRY AS PRESIDENT FOR SUCH A SHORT WHILE HAS LEFT MAGNIFICENT IMPRINT ON THE PAGES OF HISTORY HIS DEDICATION TO PEACE AND JUSTICE AND HIS ENERGETIC EFFORT TO ACHIEVE THESE ENDS PLACES HIM BESIDE THE GREATEST OUR COUNTRY AND THE WORLD WILL LONG REMEMBER HIM
THE EBENEZER BAPTIST CHURCH
PASTOR REV AND MRS M L KING SR AND DR AND MRS MARTIN LUTHER KING JR

Five

THE WRITTEN WORD

*J*ack Kennedy and the writers, newspapermen, and poets he cultivated shared a common vocabulary. After all, he had been co-
owner of a weekly newspaper in Rhode Island for several years and had
thought seriously about journalism as a career. He was personally close to
his speechwriters Sorensen and Schlesinger, and was the author of two
published books, one of which, *Profiles in Courage,* won the Pulitzer Prize.
He read the papers voraciously and took a personal interest in all the reporters who covered him. Like all presidents, he was frustrated when he
couldn't control press coverage, though many historians think he did a
better job at it than nearly any President before or since.

When he was angry at a particular journalist or publication, Kennedy
did not hesitate to show it. Once, peeved at a story, he canceled all White
House subscriptions to the *New York Herald Tribune.* He followed specific
columnists and journalists and claimed "not to read" others, even onetime mentors like former *New York Times* Washington Bureau Chief
Arthur Krock. He liked to threaten print journalists with the growing
influence of television, telling *Newsweek* Washington Bureau Chief Ben

Bradlee: "I always said that when we don't have to go through you bastards, we can really get our story over to the American people."

JFK enjoyed an especially close relationship with Phil Graham, publisher of *The Washington Post*. At the time, the *Post* was expanding its influence, having just overtaken the rival *Washington Star* in circulation. Until shortly before the 1960 Democratic Convention, Graham had been a Lyndon Johnson supporter. At the convention his intervention with LBJ was critical in convincing the future Vice President to accept as genuine Jack Kennedy's pro forma offer to share the ticket with him. For most of Kennedy's term in office, Graham enjoyed direct telephone access to the Oval Office and took a personal interest in the success of the administration.

Unfortunately, Graham also suffered from manic depression and delusional spells and refused to undergo drug treatments. In August of 1963 he used one of his hunting guns to commit suicide while on a weekend leave from the sanatorium where he was being treated. Kennedy wrote two messages of sympathy to Graham's widow, Katharine, who would become the *Post*'s new publisher; Jackie sent an eight-page letter. Some three months later, Katharine Graham was in *Newsweek*'s New York headquarters conducting a review of the "cultural" sections of the magazine with close Kennedy advisers Arthur Schlesinger and John Kenneth Galbraith when the three heard about Kennedy's assassination; the group immediately took the shuttle to Washington and went to the White House.

If the Washington press corps felt like friendly home turf to Jack Kennedy, the New York media world presented a distinctly more complex challenge. Kennedy felt that the columns of the *New York Times*'s Washington Bureau Chief James "Scotty" Reston were dull. And when his favorite *Times* reporter in Washington, Bill Lawrence, failed to persuade his bosses to send him along to cover Kennedy's 1961 parlay with Khrushchev, Kennedy and his press secretary, Pierre Salinger, helped arrange for his new job as a television journalist with ABC News.

President Kennedy leaving a press conference in the State Department Auditorium on March 21, 1963. *Abbie Rowe, White House/JFK Library*

Nevertheless, the tradition of cordial personal relationships that had existed for over a century between American presidents and the publishers of *The New York Times* continued during the Kennedy years, as evidenced by the several letters the owners sent Mrs. Kennedy. Chairman of the Board Arthur Hays Sulzberger wrote about this "sad, sad thing that has come to all of us and particularly to you and your little family." President and publisher Arthur Ochs ("Punch") Sulzberger, declared that "None of us will ever forget the great privilege of having known your husband." Iphigene Ochs Sulzberger, the matriarch of the Ochs Sulzberger clan that ran *The Times,* also sent her love, with special appreciation for the late President's "kindness and consideration of me." Most affecting, however, was the letter from Marian Sulzberger Dryfoos, widow of Orvil Dryfoos, Iphigene's

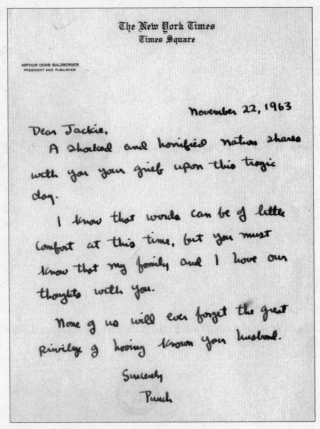

From Arthur Ochs "Punch" Sulzberger, president and publisher of *The New York Times*.

son-in-law and the man who had steered the paper during the crucial years of Jack Kennedy's candidacy and early administration. Dryfoos, weakened by the stress endured during the bitter 1963 labor dispute between New York newspaper publishers and the city's printers' union, had fallen ill shortly after it ended, and died in the hospital near the end of May.

ع✒ *Marian Sulzberger (Mrs. Orvil) Dryfoos, Director of Special Activities,* New York Times; *handwritten letter*

Nov. 27, 1963

Dear Mrs. Kennedy

. . . If only in your hours of grief I could do for you what the President did for me at the time of Orvil's death. He sent me by special messenger a handwritten letter telling me how he felt about Orv and what Orvil had done for his country. I have often reread it and it is something I shall always cherish. I am so proud to have had a part in Orv's too short, but wonderful life. I know you must feel this way too about your husband for he was really an extraordinary man, warm, sympathetic and understanding. I saw him only last Monday in Miami and in the sea of people, he remembered so many by name and had a word for each of us. . . .

Pardon me for telling you of my loss, but somehow last Friday was like six months ago and with both of these wonderful men went a part of me.

Your courage is an inspiration to all of us. . . .

My deepest sympathy
Sincerely,
Marian Dryfoos

Admiration of President Kennedy at *The New York Times* was not restricted to the publishers.

ع✒ *Joseph Loftus, reporter,* New York Times; *handwritten letter*

Nov. 30

Dear Mrs. Kennedy:

For a newspaperman trying to remain objective, Jack and Jacqueline Kennedy were a challenge that few people would understand. I know from something he said once that he thought I was a rather odd fellow. He never knew that he just charmed me into silence. This is no way for a newspaperman to behave, so I tended to avoid him, which, of course, was a poor alternative, professionally and personally. I shall regret all my life that I never let him know my tremendous admiration for him. Let me say the same of you while I still have the chance. The way you have borne this indescribable wound is beyond my ability to understand. To say that all of us would take on your burden if we could would vastly understate the case. Please believe that you have our love.

Sincerely
Joe Loftus

Jack Kennedy's high regard for working members of the press was not shared by his wife, Jacqueline. In some ways this is surprising, since after all it was Jackie, not Jack, who put in a brief stint in daily journalism when she worked as the "Inquiring Camera Girl" for the *Washington Times-Herald*. Also, Jackie clearly enjoyed her and Jack's close relationship with two Washington journalist couples: *Chattanooga Times* reporter Charles Bartlett and his wife, Martha (who had actually first brought Jack and Jackie together), and *Newsweek*'s Ben Bradlee and his wife, Toni. Socializing with journalists, however, was something else from providing them with material. Jackie made most reporters who were doing their job feel like intruders—especially women wire service reporters Helen Thomas (UPI) and Frances Lewine (AP), who were expected by their employers to shadow her every movement. True, for Helen Thomas the assignment meant calling Pierre Salinger once at three o'clock in the morning to see if it was true that one of Caroline Kennedy's hamsters had died. For someone like Jackie, who valued quiet time alone, these kinds of intrusions could be insupportable, and she sometimes responded caustically. Once, for example, when

PRESS ROOM
THE WHITE HOUSE
WASHINGTON

Dear Mrs. Kennedy,

There are no words to express the sorrow and great loss we all feel.

The President inspired us all and made us all feel that the world could be better and we should try to make it so for all people.

You both made a great contribution to history when you lived in the White House and I doubt that it will ever be as brilliant again.

Sincerely,
Helen Thomas

From Helen Thomas, UPI White House correspondent.

asked about what she planned to feed her new German shepherd puppy, she answered, straight-faced: "Reporters."

In the end, Jacqueline Kennedy succeeded brilliantly at getting favorable coverage from women's interest reporters, and even made her peace with the wire service ladies. Winzola McLendon, social reporter of *The Washington Post,* termed Mrs. Kennedy's White House projects "priceless gifts to the nation." Molly Thayer, a friend of Jacqueline's mother's who had published a genteel, more-or-less authorized biography of Jackie as JFK took office, declared in a condolence note that her subject had more than fulfilled Thayer's characterization of her three years earlier as "the most respected, most admired, and most loved First Lady in history." More than most, journalists seemed to realize that their letters of sympathy also served as good-bye missives to a memorable epoch.

If only, wrote Frances Lewine sympathetically to the bereaved First Lady, she could "unwrite this chapter of history." Helen Thomas, who broke so many of the barriers holding back women reporters of "general news," was also appreciative. Many professional women hoped that Jacqueline Kennedy would soon assume a role in the workplace, among them Dorothy Schiff of the *New York Post,* a German Jewish onetime debutante and New York's first female publisher.

❧ *Dorothy Schiff, publisher of the* New York Post; *typewritten letter*

November 29, 1963

Dear Mrs. Kennedy:

I share the grief of so many millions . . . and their admiration and respect for you. . . .

Last spring I had a half hour's conversation with your husband that I want so much to tell you about. He spoke several times of you and I want you to know what he said.

After a few weeks, I shall try to get in touch with you to see if we can meet. Work has meant so much to me in my life, and I have an idea that might interest you on that subject. . . .

Sincerely,
Dorothy Schiff

David Wise, the *Herald Tribune*'s White House correspondent, once incurred the President's wrath for highlighting the President's own remark that he, like John Quincy Adams, spent many days away from the Executive Mansion.

🖙 *David Wise, chief of the Washington Bureau of the* New York Herald Tribune; *handwritten note*

Washington, DC
November 27, 1963

Dear Mrs. Kennedy,

Once, on a lovely day in Cape Cod, you told me that your husband was a thoroughbred. In the past five days you have joined him in showing the nation and the world what the word means.

You have helped all of us, and your own loss is no less personal because you must share it with so many.

David Wise

Philip Geyelin and his wife, Sherry, had had a long personal acquaintance with Jackie's sister Lee.

🖙 *Phil Geyelin, foreign correspondent of* The Wall Street Journal *and future managing editor of* The Washington Post, *and his wife, Sherry; handwritten note*

My dearest Jackie

You crystallize like a diamond all that he stood for.

The two of you showed us what heights could be reached—and you

Jackie are showing us how those heights can be maintained. Could you possibly give him a more fitting tribute?

Our love and our pride for you both is forever. . . .

                                                              Phil & Sherry

Kennedy's adversarial relationship with Time, Inc.'s Henry and Clare Booth Luce and *Time* magazine's conservative managing editor, Otto Fuerbringer, prompted him to actively promote the rival *Newsweek*. Representatives of both newsweeklies sent Jacqueline Kennedy expressions of sympathy. *Newsweek* managing editor Osborn Elliott, who had recently broken tradition by printing bylines on news stories, sent a telegram on behalf of all his editors. Time, Inc., president James Linen sent a three-paragraph personal letter recognizing that the "anguish and grief" felt by him and his associates "can only be a tiny fragment of yours." One of *Time*'s reporters whom Kennedy did like (who published a favorable book about the President before his death) was Hugh Sidey. In his letter to the President's widow, Sidey credited JFK with "the rekindled strength of the country."

Conservative columnists were sometimes surprisingly close to the President—the gentlemanly Rowland Evans, for example, and his wife, Katherine. Until 1963 Rowly Evans had worked solo as Capitol Hill correspondent for the *New York Herald Tribune,* but had recently been paired up with the rather scruffy *Wall Street Journal* reporter Robert Novak.

≥ *Rowland Evans Jr., co-columnist of "Inside Report"; handwritten letter*

                                                         December 1, 1963

Dear Jackie—

On her way to the East Wing today to help with the mail, Katherine's cabdriver told her his wife was about to have a baby. If it's a boy, he told his wife it would be named John.

Yes, the wife said, that's what I want too—but if it's a girl it's going to be named Jacqueline.

By the time the cabdriver got to the East Wing, Katherine had told him why she was going there. And he said, "Lady, I want to carry you free, I'm not going to take your fare." And then he spoke the line that, in its plain and artless image, evoked what the President meant to so many Americans.

"Lady, Jack Kennedy had class and he made me think I had class too."

Dear Jackie, I don't have any words to say it better. I remember in the summer of 1961, when you gave us supper one evening in Hyannisport, I had just finished a magazine article on the President's humor. Well, he said, what are you going to write next? And he spent five minutes thinking up ideas, wonderfully imaginative ideas, to help us sell another magazine article.

You know how much I loved him, and how inexpressibly proud and fortunate I am, and Katherine too, to have known him at least a little. All our feelings are now for you and our country.

Affectionately,
Rowly

The admiration of some journalists, even liberal ones, was not always returned. Syndicated columnist Jim Bishop so irritated Jackie with what she considered his intrusive research at the White House for his book *One Day in the Life of President Kennedy* (though in tone it is in fact quite deferential) that she immediately ruled out collaborating with him on a book about the assassination.

Jim Bishop, syndicated columnist for King Features, future author of The Day Kennedy Was Shot

December 3, 1963

Dear Mrs. Kennedy:

Kelly and I waited until now because we are numb. Our words limp with hurt. None of them are strong enough to transmit to you. . . . Kelly's impulse was to rush to your side, as though anything she might say or do could be of the slightest assistance to a woman who has lost the love of her life. . . .

I had to say no. We could not add to the crushing burden you shouldered with a gallantry which is now historic. . . . But commiseration is worthless. . . . The intentions are noble, but the effect is to hone and re-hone the knife of grief. . . .

The pontificating of the politicians and the priests are as hail on tin. The tears of the people make you feel sorry for them, because you know, better than they, the manner of man they lost. Nothing assuages except to walk once more up that desolate hill to the little fence and to feel the nearness of him once more. . . .

Kelly and I feel deeply for you and for your husband and for Caroline and John. We left the White House with this feeling—a little shy of affection, a little more than admiration—and the passing of the President has not changed it. . . . Nothing will ever change it.

Sincerely,
Jim Bishop

In publishers' offices outside the Eastern corridor, sentiments about the Kennedys had often been less than enthusiastic, but there was little indication of this in the messages received by Jacqueline Kennedy. Marshall

Field, publisher of the populist and progressive *Chicago Sun-Times,* hailed the late President as "among this country's immortal leaders." "Prayers and sympathetic thoughts" came from Austine and Will Hearst Jr., son of the legendary newspaper tycoon William Randolph Hearst, who had been one of Joseph Kennedy Sr.'s most prized friends in the news business. Otis Chandler, the last in a long family line to serve as publisher of the *Los Angeles Times* and largely credited with transforming it from a deeply conservative regional publication to a national one respected for nonpartisan coverage, apparently felt obligated to point out that his newspaper, despite its recent endorsements of Richard Nixon, "nevertheless supported your husband in many of his programs."

And although Kennedy was roundly criticized by many progressives for purging his foreign policy team of such liberals as Chester Bowles and Richard Goodwin, he could be protective of government employees when he wanted to be. One State Department employee was effusively grateful for the way the President did just that, defending him against insinuating questions from Texas syndicated journalist Sarah McClendon.

ॐ *J. Clayton Miller; handwritten letter*

January 26, 1964

My dear Mrs. Kennedy:

Two years ago today your husband, in a press conference, denied the charge of a correspondent that another member of the Department of State and myself were "well-known security risks." His angry reaction to such an unsupported contention has stood up inviolate.

That I have a special place for him in my humble memory is something that I want you to know. That his support of me was never found to be misplaced is a matter of dignified pride.

God bless you,

J. Clayton Miller

John F. Kennedy's affection for the printed word went far beyond the daily press room. An avid reader of history, and spy novels like Ian Fleming's James Bond series, he also enlisted the most prominent poets and authors to speak at the White House and at national ceremonies. The literary world returned the admiration. The message from publishing legend Bennett Cerf was directed more particularly to Jacqueline Kennedy's recent conduct:

2• *Bennett Cerf, President of Random House; handwritten note*

November 28, 1963

Dear Mrs. Kennedy:

I must add this note of mine to the thousands you undoubtedly are receiving in similar vein to tell you how magnificent you have been all through this appalling event.

The memory of your behavior—and that of your wonderful children—will be an inspiration to my family, me—and millions of other Americans for years to come. . . .

Bennett Cerf

President Kennedy cultivated personal friendships with two of America's distinguished elderly poets, Robert Frost and Carl Sandburg. Frost, who spoke at Kennedy's inauguration, predeceased Kennedy by nearly a year. Sandburg himself was not in good health at the time of the President's death, and relied on his literary agent to relay his feelings to Mrs. Kennedy.

🐚 *Lucy Kroll, literary agent; typewritten letter*

New York, NY

Dear Mrs. Kennedy,

. . . It has been my honor to represent Carl Sandburg. He has shared with me his deep feeling about the greatness of your husband. When the news of the tragedy came to his home in North Carolina, he said to his wife that the whole world would mourn this president, and he turned to his work on Lincoln for contemplation.

I was in constant contact with Mr. Sandburg and his wife, Paula. She told me that they both felt that the poem Carl had written, WHEN DEATH CAME APRIL TWELVE, 1945, in memory of Roosevelt, was appropriate and true now and reflected their strong feeling for President Kennedy. I am enclosing the poem and I use the last two stanzas as a message from my heart to you.

> *Can a bell ring proud in the heart*
> *over a voice yet lingering*
> *over a face past any forgetting,*
> *over a shadow alive and speaking*
> *over echoes and lights come keener, come deeper?*
>
> *Can a bell ring in the heart*
> *in time with the tall headlines,*
> *the high fidelity transmitters,*
> *the somber consoles rolling sorrow,*
> *the choirs in ancient laments - chanting:*
> *"Dreamer, sleep deep,*
> *Toiler, sleep long,*

Fighter, be rested now,
Commander, sweet good night."

Most sincerely,
Lucy Kroll

A more controversial poet also sent greetings—Ezra Pound, the influential American modernist expatriate who had made radio broadcasts for Mussolini and was remanded to St. Elizabeth's mental hospital after the war. Released partly due to the influence of artist friends like Robert Frost and Igor Stravinsky, he was living back in Italy on November 22.

❧ *Ezra Pound, poet; telegram*

MRS JACQUELINE KENNEDY
GREAT GRIEF TO ALL MEN OF GOOD WILL HEARTFELT
CONDOLENCES GREAT MAN AND PRESIDENT
EZRA POUND

The following plaintive letter sent by the left-leaning Irish dramatist and autobiographer Sean O'Casey to Rose Russell of the New York Teachers Union reached Mrs. Kennedy's secretary as a telegram the day after Kennedy's funeral:

❧ *Sean O'Casey, Irish playwright; letter to Rose Russell*

St. Marychurch, Torquay, Devon
25 Nov. 1963

Miss Rose Russell,

Oh, my dear Rose,

What a terrible thing has happened to us all! To you there, to us here, to all everywhere. Peace who was becoming bright-eyed now sits in the shadow of death: her handsome champion has been killed as he walked by her very side. Her gallant boy is dead.

What a cruel, foul, and most unnatural murder!

We mourn here with you poor, sad American People

Sean

In his brief telegram, African-American poet and playwright Langston Hughes mourned the "great and beloved American for whom I among millions grieve." Another great African-American literary figure, the Pulitzer Prize–winning poet Gwendolyn Brooks, sent her *Chicago Sun-Times* editor Emmett Dedmon the following poem, which he both published and sent along to Mrs. Kennedy in original manuscript form:

❧ *Gwendolyn Brooks, Pulitzer Prize—winning poet; typed poem*

THE ASSASSINATION OF JOHN KENNEDY

> . . . this good, this Decent,
> this Kindly man . . .
> —Senator Mansfield

I hear things crying in the world.
A nightmare congress of obscure
Delirium uttering overbreath
The tilt and jangle of this death.

Who had a sense of world and man,
Who had an apt and antic grace
Lies lenient, lapsed and large beneath
The tilt and jangle of this death.

The world goes on with what it has.
Its reasoned, right and only code.
Coaxing, with military faith,
The tilt and jangle of this death.

Gwendolyn Brooks
Friday, November 22, 1963

Six

HOLLYWOOD AND THE JET SET

*A*merica in the fall of 1963 was a world from another era. There were only three television networks. Nine of the top ten shows were broadcast on CBS (only *Bonanza,* in second place, gave NBC an in-road). Gas was thirty cents a gallon, milk a little higher at forty-nine cents. The choices offered at movie theaters included *From Russia with Love,* the latest James Bond; Alfred Hitchcock's *The Birds;* and *Cleopatra,* the film that brought Elizabeth Taylor international fame, along with the condemnation of the Vatican for her affair with Richard Burton during filming.

The Kennedy presidency was a pivotal period in cultural terms as well as social and political ones. The long decline of the European aristocratic order came as a new American middle class began to adopt more sophisticated values. The new Kennedy ethos was both meritocratic and elitist. Jackie Kennedy brought a world of refinement to Washington—and in the process made the White House a performance venue and national salon for writers, actors, artists, and intellectuals. Adopting the conventions of an age when newspapers ran most of their arts coverage on the Women's, Society, and Fashion pages, Mrs. Kennedy ended up elevating questions of style and beauty into topics of serious conversation.

The Kennedy White House became a showcase, as White House dinners mixed key figures from vastly disparate worlds. The White House state dinner welcoming Grand Duchess Charlotte of Luxembourg, for example, was also used to honor Mayor Richard Daley of Chicago—whose reputation as a political boss carried more than a whiff of corruption. Daley stayed as a personal guest in the White House, while the royal party was put up in Blair House. Why the special treatment? social secretary Letitia Baldrige inquired of JFK. Because, he replied, "I wouldn't be President if it weren't for him." The Grand Duchess, who in London exile had become a symbol of national resistance during the World War II German occupation, wrote Mrs. Kennedy how "deeply shocked" she and her family were to "learn of the terrible accident of President Kennedy."

Intermarriages and the exchange of loyalties across the oceans had accelerated since the end of World War II. The alliance between Hollywood and European nobility, symbolically celebrated in the 1956 marriage between Prince Rainier of Monaco and the actress and society figure Grace Kelly, was also celebrated in Washington only a few months after the Kennedy inauguration by an informal luncheon at the White House in honor of the Prince and Princess.

❧ *Prince Rainier of Monaco; telegram*

MONTECARLO NOV 22 2350
MRS JOHN FITZGERALD KENNEDY
PRINCESS GRACE AND I ARE MOST PROFOUNDLY
SHOCKED AND SADDENED BY THE NEWS OF THE
TRAGIC DEATH OF THE PRESIDENT STOP YOUR GRIEV-
OUS LOSS IS SHARED AND MOURNED BY THE PRINCESS
AND MYSELF AND BY THE ENTIRE PEOPLE OF
MONACO . . .
RAINIER PRINCE OF MONACO

Another cosmopolitan acquaintance of Mrs. Kennedy's was "Loulou" de Vilmorin, a French novelist and poet whose husbands and lovers included Antoine de Saint-Exupéry, two Hungarian counts, a British ambassador, the French Minister of Culture, and the Las Vegas millionaire Henry Leigh Hunt.

๛ *Louise Levêque de Vilmorin, writer and companion of French Minister of Culture André Malraux; handwritten note, in French*

Verriéres-le-Buisson

23 November 1963

Chère Madame,

Quelle horreur! Quel drame! Quel chagrin! La mort désastreuse du Président Kennedy désole le monde entier et me porte vers vous dans un élan de profonde sympathie. Votre malheur est dans mon cœur. Je pense à vous sans cesse et je suis très fidèlement votre

Louise de Vilmorin

Dear Madame,

What horror! What tragedy! What anguish! The disastrous death of President Kennedy desolates the entire world and carries me towards you in a surge of profound sympathy. Your misfortune is in my heart. I think of you without ceasing and am faithfully

your

Louise de Vilmorin

During her years of marriage to Jack, Jackie relied heavily on her sister Lee for real personal support and understanding. Lee in turn introduced her sister to some of the British aristocratic circles in which she was circulating after her move to England with first husband Michael Canfield and subsequent marriage to Polish Prince Stanislas Radziwill. Messages of sympathy that reflected these associations streamed into the White House from most of the royal families left in the world. Several of these had long since lost their kingdoms or principalities, like King Leka I of Albania; Margarita, Queen of Bulgaria; and the King and Queen of Yugoslavia. A politically more significant figure of exiled royalty, Nicolai Alexandrovich Romanoff—one of the two pretenders to the Czar Nicholas II's abolished throne of Russia—sent his condolences on "behalf of all the exiled Russians in the United Kingdom."

Besides aristocratic social connections, Jackie's sister Lee encouraged her interest in clothes. Back at Jacqueline Kennedy's 1947 debutante party, younger sister Lee had emerged in a racy outfit that outshone the more demure Jackie, who determined not to be outshone again. Still, using connections formed from early work at *Harper's Bazaar* and *Vogue,* Lee often acted as her older sister's mentor in matters of style. Jackie's effectiveness as the candidate's fashion plate wife became clear during the 1960 campaign. Ambassador Joe decided that he would foot the big bills—as long as the designer was an American. Unsurprisingly, the man tapped for the job was

Oleg Cassini, an old Kennedy family friend whose Russian grandfather, Count Arthur Cassini, had worked with Theodore Roosevelt to negotiate the end of the Russo-Japanese War. At the Kennedy White House he had found perhaps the nearest equivalent—"in style, at least—to a royal court." Cassini's ambition was to create a certain tone for the new administration—"simple, youthful, but magisterial elegance." Cassini determined to have a hand in helping create "an American Versailles." He and Jackie exchanged playful, slightly campy notes about her role, with her instructing him to concentrate on designing daytime outfits "that I would wear if Jack were President of FRANCE—*très Princessse de Rethy mais jeune. . . .*" On November 22 Oleg Cassini sent his most important client a telegram, which he soon followed with a letter.

⁊ *Oleg Cassini; handwritten note*

Dearest Jackie

There are no words to describe my feelings of horror and loss, and there are no words to describe how much I and everyone else admires you.

Whenever you shall have a moment in the future I should love to come and pay my respects. It is a very small thing indeed but if you wish I would be honored to continue for you in my humble role.

Yours devotedly,
Oleg

Oleg Cassini was no doubt the principal organizer of the "Jackie" look presented to the world during the thousand days of the Kennedy White House. But picking out the names of apparel designers, retailers, and manufacturers from those who signed telegrams and letters of consolation gives rise to a kind of honor roll of the larger world of sixties high style: dressmaker Marguerite Paul; French hat designer Lily Daché and her husband, Coty executive Jean Despres; Andrew Goodman of Bergdorf Goodman and Stanley Marcus of Neiman Marcus; Marc Bohan of the house of Dior; Los Angeles designer Gustave Tassell; the recently discovered Dominican designer and Balenciaga protégé Oscar de la Renta; as well as a telegram and letter from the one foreign house of design whose clothes the First Lady explicitly acknowledged wearing (but only when in Paris, in deference to her hosts): Givenchy.

The televised White House tour had made Jackie Kennedy into a household name. Less well known was the French interior decorator who became largely responsible for the overall redesign.

₰ *Stéphane Boudin, decorator, head of Maison Jansen; handwritten letter, in French*

1st December 1963

My poor dear Jacqueline

. . . And so end those happy days where you and I attempted to create a little bit of beauty in this residence, before us so impersonal, and it's a small consolation to hope that the future cannot erase the imprint made, in passing through, by the wonderful couple you were. As for me, it's a unique page in my life . . . since I cannot believe, dear Jackie, that I will be so fortunate that you might have need of me. Otherwise you know well that, as in the beginning in the little house in Washington, I will come running to prove to you all my faithful affection.

Very sadly and for always your
Stéphane Boudin

With the Kennedy fortune on her husband's side and the Bouvier/ Auchincloss pedigree on the other, it's no wonder that hundreds of the socially dominant "right people" were among those who sent letters of sympathy to Mrs. Kennedy—including the heirs and captains among the great American industrialists. Amory "Amo" Houghton Jr., who would soon become Chairman and CEO of Corning Glass and later a U.S. Congressman, was acquainted with Jacqueline "from college days." In a brief letter sent in mid-December, he praised her for being "valiant and exemplary . . . through a period of crushing sorrow." Betty and Harvey Firestone talked of "your grievous loss" and "the loss to our country and to the world." Anne McDonnell Ford, an old Kennedy family friend, sent a telegram with "assurance of our prayers"; in his wire, Cornelius Vanderbilt Jr. was "shocked and stunned." George Getty II's letter affirmed that the memory of JFK "will always shine brightly." Two of the socially well-connected Cushing sisters, Betsey Whitney and Babe Paley, both wrote to Jackie. The first had been an occasional White House hostess during her marriage to James Roosevelt and afterward forged an important partnership with *New York Herald Tribune* publisher John Hay Whitney; she was "stunned at the staggering realization that we have lost our great President." Her sister, a former fashion editor and onetime spouse of Standard Oil heir Stanley Mortimer, currently married to CBS titan William Paley, wrote from Long Island:

᭞ *Babe Paley; handwritten letter*

Kiluna Farm
Manhasset, New York

Dear Jackie—

I have no words to express my sense of bereavement at this most appalling tragedy. The world is in tears at the loss of the dynamic young genius who didn't have a chance to finish the job. . . .

And you have been an inspiration and example for all. . . .

You have my deepest sympathy and affection.

Babe Paley

The President and First Lady fostered a commitment to science and the arts greater than that of any of their predecessors, and tours abroad by American arts groups became a key part of this cultural outreach. One was led by the African-American conductor Henry Lewis and his wife, opera singer Marilyn Horne (nicknamed "Jackie" by people who knew her). One of the musicians on that tour was violinist Spiro Stamos:

ᘏ *Katherine and Spiro Stamos; handwritten letters*

Jan. 25, 1964

Dear Mrs. Kennedy,

My husband sent me this letter when he was in Trondheim, Norway, on Nov. 22nd when he was on tour with the Los Angeles Chamber Orchestra.

He expressed in words what I felt in my heart & I feel I would like to share this with you. . . .

Respectfully,
Katherine Stamos

Britannia Hotel
Trondheim, Norway
Nov. 22, 1963

My dearest wife—

This is one of the darkest moments of my life—tonight as we were awaiting Henry to come on-stage between the pieces during a concert—there was a great delay—then finally he and Jackie came on and started an aria—we played about 1 minute then he stopped and said "I can't go on anymore—President Kennedy has been assassinated."—Then next thing I knew I was crying, as if I lost my own brother or father—but more than our own personal loss—we have lost our leader, our hope for a better world within our own lifetime. They did the same thing to Christ, to Lincoln—

and now Kennedy—may God help us in this hour of great darkness—our faith must be strong as Kennedy's was. He took the chance—to try and reform the hidden ignorance, the bigotry of the past and now he has become a martyr. He had touched our own personal lives—*I would not be here if it weren't for Kennedy*, trying to show the world that we are a cultured people. But some of us aren't—as long as we have fanaticism to have produced such a dastardly deed. . . .

Keep up your spirit—I'll be home soon.

Your husband,
Spiro

A favorite book among intellectuals of the day was British writer C. P. Snow's *The Two Cultures and the Scientific Revolution,* which bemoaned the lack of understanding between scientists and those involved in the arts and humanities. The Kennedys promoted dialogue and mutual enrichment between the groups by determinedly mixing them at White House events. One of the most celebrated of these was the April 29, 1962, dinner for Nobel Prize Laureates at which Kennedy paid special tribute to Thomas Jefferson's many-leveled intellect. One of the Nobel Laureates who attended that dinner sent the following condolences to Mrs. Kennedy:

᠊᠊ᴥ *Dr. Fritz Lipmann, Nobel Prize–winning German-American biochemist; handwritten note*

The Rockefeller Institute
New York, NY
December 23, 1963

Dear Mrs. Kennedy:

One has been in a daze and torpor, it has been so difficult to collect one's thoughts. And then one felt, why add still one more to the overwhelming flow of letters. Yet it makes me unhappy not . . . to send a message, having been one of the fortunate guests at your Nobel dinner in 1962. We were so gracefully received it left . . . a shiningly bright remembrance, which we cherish.

Now as it is over so suddenly, one grasps grievingly the irretrievable loss of a unique President. Unique he was, particularly for the fringe who, as he did in politics, strive for the new and novel in science and arts. Our world has suddenly become so gray. . . .

Most sincerely yours,
Fritz Lipmann

Dr. Albert Schweitzer, Nobel Peace Prize winner of 1952 and one of the founders of the Committee for a Sane Nuclear Policy, sent Mrs. Kennedy this letter from the hospital he established in equatorial Africa:

❧ *Dr. Albert Schweitzer, eighty-eight-year-old French-German doctor and theologian; handwritten letter in French*

Lambaréné, Gabon
8 December 1963

Madame

I want to tell you what respect and friendship I felt for your husband the President. He was a noble personage. He had the will to make the most of the duty which devolved on him from the high position he occupied.

He was a great and noble President. Thus will he enter history.

I admire him particularly because he had the courage to search for a solution to the agonizing problem of atomic weapons. On this issue he put us on the right path.

He was a blessing not only for his homeland but for the entire world. . . .

Your devoted Albert Schweitzer

Less than a fortnight after the assassination, President Lyndon B. Johnson awarded thirty-one outstanding citizens of the world the Presidential Medal of Freedom. The honorees had been selected and the award itself basically conceived by President Kennedy. Photographer Edward Steichen, who had curated the famous *Family of Man* photography exhibit at the Museum of Modern Art, was among those honored.

Kate Steichen, daughter of Edward Steichen; handwritten Christmas card enclosing one small box of frankincense and myrrh

My dear Mrs. Kennedy—

For many years, to many children, I have given this real *Frankincense* and real *Myrrh*—and this year of all my years, I yearn to send some to John and Caroline. You yourself have the real *Gold*—in the children themselves, as God knows. This, then, is my small salute to you—as a charter member of The Family of Man.

May I please sign: Love,
Kate

The photographer and set and costume designer Cecil Beaton kept a lively diary in which he described the intimate London dinner party for Jackie given by Jakie and Chiquita Astor during her London visit in June 1961. Two years later, when he first heard about the assassination, he noted: "My blood turned to a pale liquid; I felt I was rushing through space down a lift shaft." Ten days later, more composed, he wrote as follows:

~ *Cecil Beaton; handwritten letter*

December 2nd

Dear Jackie,

I haven't written before this because I haven't known how to create words that would be suitable. Even now there is no way of expressing the terrible sadness I feel to what has happened. It's one of the most cruel strokes of fate that has ever befallen anyone in my lifetime. It's more shocking and unaccountable than anything I remember.

Such a useless waste makes the whole world poorer, and for you it must be the most agonizing loss. There is nothing your friends can do except to grieve with you and send sympathy—this I do with all my heart.

Yours affectionately,

Cecil Beaton

Jacqueline Kennedy's fondness for opera and ballet and the performing arts dated back to her early youth, when she assembled a library about ballet and dreamed about designing costumes for the theater. Jack Kennedy, according to his daughter, Caroline, didn't like the ballet, and would make "faces when he thinks no one is looking." Nonetheless, he gave his wife free rein to bring all kinds of music to the White House. According to Arthur Schlesinger, Igor Stravinsky felt so comfortable at the small 1962 White House dinner in his honor that he leaned over to Schlesinger and whispered in his ear, "I am drunk." The famous state dinner at which the renowned Catalan cellist Pablo Casals performed also brought to the White House many of America's most significant composers (among them Samuel Barber, Elliott Carter, Aaron Copland, Gian Carlo Menotti, Virgil Thomson, and Leonard Bernstein).

Accordingly, prominent composers and conductors were quick to send

The Kennedys greet the Stravinskys before the White House dinner in Stravinsky's honor on January 18, 1962. *Abbie Rowe, White House/JFK Library*

condolences to Mrs. Kennedy. Stravinsky and his wife, Vera, "shocked and heartbroken," sent a telegram of "deep-felt compassion" from Rome; the composer also wrote an "Elegy for JFK," scored for voice and three clarinets. Douglas Moore, composer of *The Devil and Daniel Webster,* credited Mr. and Mrs. Kennedy with bringing closer "the day when music, painting, poetry and sculpture will be truly a part of the bloodstream of American life." Rudolf Bing, head of the Metropolitan Opera, wired recalling the president's "efforts in our behalf." Risë Stevens, the same company's star mezzo-soprano, praised the first couple's "patronage of the arts and artists" that "brought new vitality to the nation's culture."

One of Jackie's first guests in the White House, the choreographer George Balanchine, sent a telegram in which he "deeply grieved over the tragic loss." From London, Frederick Ashton, the ballet master of the Royal

ANTAL DORATI
Via dei Foraggi 74
Rome

London, 23.11.63

Dear Mrs. Kennedy,

Shocked, grieved, outraged,
humiliated beyond any
means of expression, —
may I tell you, one voice
amongst millions, — that
my heart goes out to
you in your grief in the
most deeply felt sym-
pathy.

Nothing more can be
said now that would be
more than repetition of
words, sincere, but su-
perfluous.

It will be proven by
deeds rather than words.

that your husband lived
bravely for great values.
Be assured that many men
will try to do their best to
prove that.

Respectfully, yours

Antal Dorati

Ballet, wired "deepest sympathy" from all members of his troupe. Famous conductors like George Szell of the Cleveland Orchestra and Erich Leinsdorf of the Boston Symphony wrote notes of sympathy, while Antal Dorati, the Hungarian-born American conductor and composer most widely identified with a long tenure at the Minneapolis Symphony Orchestra, wrote Mrs. Kennedy that he was "shocked, grieved, outraged, humiliated beyond any means of expression."

In 1939, when Washington, D.C., was still an officially segregated city, the African-American contralto Marian Anderson was refused permission by the Daughters of the American Revolution to give a concert at Constitution Hall on the grounds that it would attract a "mixed audience" of blacks and whites. The controversy that ensued brought her international attention, and twenty years later she sang "The Star-Spangled Banner" at Kennedy's inauguration. On November 22 she wired Jacqueline Kennedy:

☙ *Marian Anderson, world-celebrated contralto; telegram*

NEW YORK NY 22 811P EST
MRS JACQUELINE KENNEDY
WORDS ARE FUTILE AT A TIME LIKE THIS. WITH A
HEAVY HEART I AM EXTENDING MY SYMPATHY AND
PRAYERS THAT GOD'S BLESSING BE UPON YOU AND
YOUR FAMILY SINCERELY
MARIAN ANDERSON

One of Jackie's closest advisers in the field of culture, Goddard Lieberson, was among those who paid their respects in the East Room on Saturday afternoon:

☙ *Goddard Lieberson, president, Columbia Records; handwritten letter*

XI

24

Dearest Jacqueline—

For those of us who love you, seeing you these days, has made us want to do the impossible, to rush to your side. . . . We did have a blessed moment . . . in the East Room on Saturday afternoon, where we could only weep in shocked disbelief. I was haunted by the final words of Jeanne d'Arc in "Jeanne au Bûcher": From her deep belief, she said: "J'accepte—j'accepte"—What else is there to say in the face of the inconceivable?

With much love   Goddard

It's tempting to read more into Goddard Lieberson's comparison of Jackie to Joan of Arc, especially in light of the fate of Queen Guinevere in *Camelot* (nearly burned at the stake until rescued by Lancelot). JFK's fondness for the 1960 Lerner and Loewe musical became common knowledge after Jackie made much of it in her Thanksgiving 1963 post-assassination interview with journalist Theodore White. No sooner had White's report appeared in *Life* magazine than it found an enthusiastic echo among admirers of the late President—as evidenced by a typed letter on *Camelot* stationery sent from the Players' Club by Robert Downing, the original production's stage manager. The *"real* CAMELOT," Downing insisted, "was in the heart and . . . great and good deeds of your husband."

Besides tunes from Broadway musicals, the President loved traditional Irish ballads as well as songs from male vocalists like Frank Sinatra and Bing Crosby. In a handwritten note, singer and actor Crosby, one of the best-known media stars of the age, wrote to Mrs. Kennedy: "We shall not see his like again on the national scene."

Both Jack and Jackie appreciated the society band music of Meyer Davis and Lester Lanin that they knew from weddings and debutante balls; both bandleaders sent condolence telegrams. Jackie, who was younger, liked to spice things up at dance parties by introducing the twist—a development JFK at first criticized as a lapse of decorum, and which indeed caused raised eyebrows among some mainstream cultural commentators.

Like other citizens, America's pop stars were shaken by the president's violent death. Wladziu Valentino Liberace, the highest-paid entertainer in the world at the time, known universally only by his last name, offered Mrs. Kennedy his "deepest sympathy in your bereavement." Frankie Laine, the pop singer who became famous for renditions of themes from movie and TV westerns like *Rawhide,* and his wife, Nann, called their single meeting with JFK the previous year in Palm Springs California the "high point of our humble lives." In their telegrams former vaudeville dancer Sammy

Dear Mrs Kennedy – My wife, Bing Kathryn, and I want very much to extend our sympathies and condolences to you because of your tragic and insupportable loss. We felt Jack Kennedy to be a brilliant, decent, dedicated man, and we both think we shall not see his like again on the national scene. Your composure courage and quiet dignity, thruout the crushing ordeal of last

weekend was a source of inspiration to the millions who watched and prayed with you.

With all sincere sentiments

Bing Crosby

Davis Sr. and Sinatra-influenced vocalist Vic Damone wished the deceased President respectively "perpetual light" and the blessing of "heavenly graces." The jazz bandleader Count Basie and his wife sent a consoling telegram from their home in St. Albans, Queens, while jazz legend Duke Ellington wired sympathies from Ankara, Turkey. Many months after the death, Pearl Bailey, overcoming her initial decision against mailing the letter, sent a message of condolence that flowed with the inflections of one of the African-American actress/singer's songs:

꿈 *Pearl Bailey Bellson; handwritten letter*

Dear Mrs. Kennedy:

. . . Your husband has departed this life—and only this life—Eternity is his.

I watched your every action on that day—yours became a "Full Face of Courage."

Dear Lady—God in all His mercy will strengthen your heart to-day—so go forth in peace . . .

Your husband has found his reward—Peace—

He was smiling—waving at a child—

He gained

   We lost

Again man as much as he doesn't sometimes like must say deep within—

There is someone

   Something

   Somewhere

Higher

Love and Keep Loving Dear Lady—God will fill your cup—Drink forever of it.

We will remain empty, dry—and alone—never sharing Your peace unless we learn the milk of human kindness.

Mrs. Pearl Bailey Bellson

The letter to the First Lady written by Josephine Baker, the expatriate African-American cabaret performer who created a sensation at the Folies

Bergère in 1920s Paris, was conceived in an inimitable blend of English and French. Baker had written JFK an admiring letter about his inaugural speech; she was also the only woman to speak at the 1963 march on Washington, where she appeared wearing her World War II Free French uniform.

≈❧ *Josephine Baker, dancer-actress-singer; handwritten letter*

le 14 Dec. 1963

Dear Mrs. Kennedy

this is not the time *de vous souhaiter les fêtes de noel* or New Year but I just could not sit here and not say a word, because I too have children, and know what it means to be alone—even if we are surrounded by thousands of people—

Alors chère chère Madame le monde entier vous aime et admire—pour votre courage et l'amour que vous avez pour vos enfants et votre cher mari; I received his letter sent on the 8th of nov 1963 in answer to mine.

Please give my most affectionate regards to all your family and to your *belle famille*

know that I am your sincere Friend in all circumstances

Josephine Baker
Village du Monde
Périgord

Since Joseph Kennedy's days in Hollywood in the 1920s, the Kennedy clan had known something about the persuasive cultural power of talking pictures and the big screen. The Kennedy connections to the Hollywood world were solidified by the 1955 marriage of Jack's sister Pat to actor Peter Lawford, who in this period could boast of such box-office film hits as *Ocean's Eleven* and *Advise and Consent,* as well as *The Thin Man* television series. Among the television superstars who saluted the President's memory in telegrams to Mrs. Kennedy were Milton Berle, George Burns, and Gracie Allen. "The nation's loss is immeasurable and yours is more," wired Hugh Downs, host of *The Today Show* and the TV quiz game *Concentration* and until 1962 announcer for Jack Paar's *Tonight Show*. "All artists are in deep mourning," wrote the veteran actress Agnes Moorehead, soon to achieve greater mass recognition as the witch Endora in the television series *Bewitched*.

    Philip Barry Jr., television producer, son of the Irish-American playwright of the same name; handwritten letter

Tuesday

Dear Jackie,

    It is seventeen years since we barely knew each other on the beaches of East Hampton. Today I know you well for my heart has been at your side for four desperate days.

And there it remains . . .
In deep sympathy,
Philip Barry, Jr.

Noël Coward was an occasional social acquaintance of the Kennedys. His succinct note to Mrs. Kennedy two days after the tragedy was heartfelt, though he and John F. Kennedy had very disparate styles. Coward admired Kennedy's "courage, comparative youth and style," but also criticized him for being "Catholic and self-willed." Kennedy, for his part, is said to have done an excellent Noël Coward imitation.

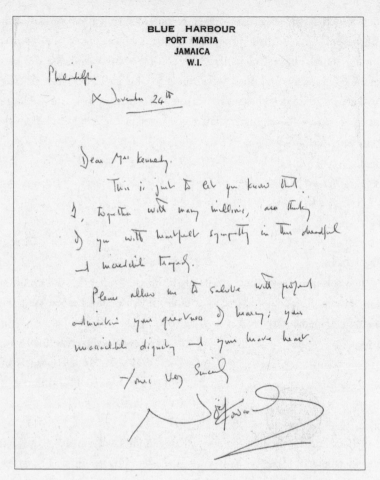

2e *Noël Coward, English playwright, composer, and director; handwritten note*

Philadelphia
November 24th

Dear Mrs Kennedy,

This is just to let you know that I, together with many millions, am thinking of you with heartfelt sympathy in this dreadful and incredible tragedy.

Please allow me to salute with profound admiration your greatness of bearing; your incredible dignity and your brave heart.

Yours very sincerely
Noël Coward

Lauren Bacall, who married actor Jason Robards several years after the death of her first husband, Humphrey Bogart, was known for her liberal political views and friendships with writers and journalists.

❧ *Lauren Bacall, screen and stage actress; handwritten letter*

Dear Mrs. Kennedy—

This letter is so difficult to write. But a day has not passed that you and your husband have not been in our thoughts. Jason and I still find the horrible hard to believe. The terror that exists in our country and the waste of a man who gave so much and had so much more. We miss him.

Our admiration for you could never be put into proper words. We wish you luck and hope you may find some happiness in your life.

We just wanted you to know that you are thought of and the passage of time has in no way lessened our feeling of loss—

with deep and fond regards
Lauren Bacall Robards

Jack Kennedy used his wit and humor effectively both as candidate and president, but it was his most successful impersonator, twenty-six-year-old comedian Vaughn Meader, who made a vocation out of it. Meader's record album, *The First Family,* became the fastest-selling LP in history after it appeared in the fall of 1962. Unfortunately, the assassination stopped record sales dead in their tracks, and Meader's career never recovered.

We just wanted you to
know that you are thought of
and the passage of time has in
no way lessened our feeling of
loss —
                    with deep and fond regards.
                    Lauren Bacall Robards

۶ *Vaughn Meader, comedian and impersonator; handwritten letter*

NYC. NY.

Dear Mrs. Kennedy,

. . . Most Americans this past week have felt as if someone from their own family had gone. To us John F. Kennedy was an older brother, strong, honest and good. . . . Although we never met, I felt as though I had known him all my life. I was given by fate, the ability to impersonate his voice & to copy his gestures. I sincerely hope that a part of what I did found its way to him and gave him and his family a few pleasant moments.

I guess as an adult I know too many words & therefore have trouble picking out the right ones. The newspapers reported that when John Jr. was told of his father's death he said "Now I have no one to play with."

Sometimes children say it right—We have lost our big brother. We must now make him proud of us.

. . . I remain

Respectfully yours,
Vaughn Meader

Many actors and actresses sent consoling letters and telegrams to Mrs. Kennedy. A selective list includes Merle Oberon, Cary Grant, Anthony Quinn, Ralph Bellamy, Tony Curtis, Gloria DeHaven, Clifton Webb, Peter Sellers, Vincent Price, Joseph Cotten, Vivien Leigh, Joan Fontaine, June Allyson and her son Dick Powell Jr., Joan Blondell (who was the elder Dick Powell's ex-wife), and Paul Newman and Joanne Woodward. The French acting couple of Yves Montand and Simone Signoret recalled pleasant memories of time passed with the President and First Lady. Gene Kelly, who had sung and danced at the White House in October during the Irish Prime Minister's visit, wired his "deepest sympathies on this sad day."

"May perpetual light shine upon your dear husband," wired Kay (Mrs. Clark) Gable. Lydia (Mrs. Charlton) Heston offered in Spanish a line from a funeral sonnet of Spanish Baroque poet Luis de Góngora y Argote: *"Tierra sella que tierra nunca oprima"* (Earth seals, that earth may no longer oppress). The author/actress Cornelia Otis Skinner wired that her heart was "bleeding" for Mrs. Kennedy. The director Elia Kazan and his wife, the playwright Molly Day Thacher, who would herself die suddenly three weeks later, found themselves "full of grief." David Niven, a superstar from his role as Phileas Fogg in the 1956 film *Around the World in Eighty Days,* along with his wife, Hjördis, had been a guest of Kennedy's both aboard the presidential yacht *Sequoia* and at Camp David. In the days after JFK's death they sent Jackie both an offer of refuge at their home in Switzerland and the following promise:

❧ *David Niven, English actor, and his wife; handwritten note*

23rd Nov.

Dearest Jackie

Just to send all our love to you and God knows if you ever feel we can help . . . we'll come running.

All love
Hjördis and David Niven

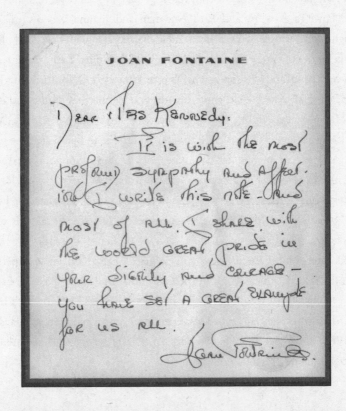

Angie Dickinson knew Jack Kennedy from the Hollywood "Rat Pack" circle of Frank Sinatra, Peter Lawford, Sammy Davis Jr., Dean Martin, Joey Bishop, and Shirley MacLaine.

ᴈ❧ *Angie Dickinson, television and movie actress; telegram*

MRS. JOHN F. KENNEDY
THE WHITE HOUSE
DEAR MRS KENNEDY WE HAVE NEVER MET BUT I CAMPAIGNED FOR PRESIDENT KENNEDY AND KNOW MOST OF THE FAMILY. THEREFORE I FELT I KNEW YOU ALSO A LITTLE. NOW I FEEL I KNOW YOU WELL, BUT NOT WELL ENOUGH NOR DOES ANYONE BUT GOD, TO RELIEVE YOU OF EVEN SOME OF YOUR GRIEF. ALTHOUGH WE GRIEVE SO DEEPLY. IN FINDING OUR HAPPIEST MOMENTS THROUGH YOUR HUSBAND, WE NOW CANNOT ESCAPE FROM OUR SADDEST MOMENTS . . .
ANGIE DICKINSON

In some ways the broad cultural vision laid out by film star Shelley Winters in the following letter to Mrs. Kennedy presaged her later career as a writer.

📪 *Shelley Winters, movie, stage, and television actress; typewritten letter*

December 3, 1963

Dear Mrs. Kennedy,

There are no adequate words that I know of, in our language, to express to you the feelings of grief that we all share with you. . . . All my friends and acquaintances (in the Actors Studio, in the theatre and in the films) know that their children are less protected and less sure of a bright future in the world now. . . .

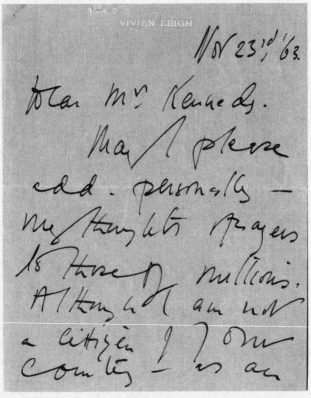

From actress Vivien Leigh.

The purpose of this letter is selfish: to remind you of the need the American people have of you and your abilities. The things which you represent and were bringing into high esteem in our national life have been terribly neglected. . . . The need in all of us for music, art, literature and the beauty and strength of our American tradition goes on. Please find a way of continuing your work. . . .

I look forward to someday meeting the woman who has made me proud to be one.

Sincerely,
Shelley Winters

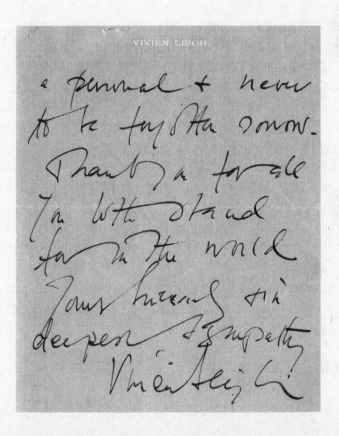

Darryl F. Zanuck sent Jacqueline Kennedy one of the longest telegrams she received (and the only fully punctuated one). Zanuck was a cofounder of 20th Century Pictures (later 20th Century Fox) who worked independently in Europe during the late 1950s and '60s before returning to Hollywood to finish production of the studio's epic *Cleopatra*.

❧ *Darryl F. Zanuck, 20th Century Fox studio executive; telegram*

DEAR MRS KENNEDY

 I WAS IN ROME WHEN THE TRAGIC ACCIDENT OC-CURRED, IN ADDITION TO MY GRIEF AND SHOCK I WAS NEVER MORE ASHAMED OF BEING AN AMERICAN. DURING THE LAST SEVERAL DAYS, AND THROUGHOUT THE FUNERAL CEREMONY, I WAS NEVER MORE PROUD OF BEING AN AMERICAN. UNDER THESE TEDIOUS CIR-CUMSTANCES YOU CONDUCTED YOURSELF IN A MAN-NER THAT GAVE NEW DIGNITY TO OUR NATION. I KNOW THAT YOU WILL BE INTERESTED TO LEARN THAT IN ROME ON THE DAY FOLLOWING THE ASSAS-SINATION ALL OF THE ADVERTISING BILLBOARDS WERE REMOVED THROUGHOUT THE CITY AND WERE REPLACED WITH LARGE BILLBOARD POSTERS WITH A FULL-SIZED PHOTOGRAPH OF OUR LATE PRESIDENT. ALL TELEVISION AND RADIO PROGRAMS WERE CAN-CELLED WITH THE EXCEPTION OF NEWS BULLETINS. THIS IS A SMALL TOKEN BUT IT IS INDICATIVE OF THE RESPECT A FOREIGN COUNTRY HELD FOR YOUR HUS-BAND. SINCERELY YOURS
DARRYL F. ZANUCK

Seven

MOURNING IN EVERY NATION

*F*oreign policy was John F. Kennedy's true metier. Since his college days he had been fascinated not only by America's place in the world, but also by the international positions of other nations. His college thesis dealt with the question of national motivation in a democratic society. Like his hero John Quincy Adams, he spent extensive time abroad when his father served as Ambassador to the United Kingdom; he had also traveled widely, often under the guidance of some of the most experienced American foreign policy hands.

Other nations and other continents more than returned young President Kennedy's interest in them. Though he had never been good at foreign languages, his youth, humor, and enthusiasm spoke for themselves. And when he traveled with the First Lady he brought along not only a cosmopolitan figure of fashion and beauty, but an accomplished linguist who conversed fluidly in several foreign languages. The White House itself became an international platform: in less than three years the Kennedys entertained seventy-four foreign leaders and hosted more than sixty state dinners and receptions.

Many Americans who wrote to Jacqueline Kennedy in November and December of 1963 cited her husband's interest and skill in dealing with other nations as a great asset. Matthew Looram, a diplomat who worked in the State Department, wrote Jackie that JFK "understood the issues" in foreign policy. And in a long letter of sympathy to Mrs. Kennedy, Mrs. M. Lejims, an interpreter in the State Department's Language Services Division, testified to the "amazing fund of knowledge and keen discernment of problems" the President displayed while she interpreted for him during exchanges with foreign leaders.

Kennedy came into office at a time of growing confrontation between the United States and Soviet Union. The shooting down of a U-2 spy plane during the last year of the Eisenhower administration, the growing radicalization of Castro's Cuban government, and an accelerating drain of Germans from the Communist part of that country all threatened to unbalance the precarious nuclear stalemate known as the Cold War. Today Cuba and Vietnam may be remembered as the main foreign flash points associated with the Kennedy presidency, but when JFK took office, the key to American interests lay squarely in Berlin—the partitioned city of once-imperial Germany in the heart of Central Europe.

West Berlin was the only "free" European urban zone behind the Iron Curtain dividing Communist from non-Communist Europe. Its survival as a Western outpost had been assured only by an intensive American-run airlift during the early years of the Cold War. The continued division of Berlin exacerbated tensions that in 1961 threatened to break out into nuclear war. The erection of the Berlin Wall in August was at first seen as a calamitous further destabilization, especially when Allied and Soviet tanks faced off momentarily at Checkpoint Charlie two months later. Over time, and especially after John F. Kennedy won the hearts of millions of Germans by declaring, *"Ich bin ein Berliner,"* the Wall proved a propaganda bonus for the West.

When news of the assassination reached Berlin on November 22, it was already evening. The student councils of the two universities in West Berlin immediately organized a spontaneous, silent, torchlit parade; with them was West Berlin Mayor and future German Chancellor Willy Brandt.

🙚 *Ernst-Josef Pauw, German student and activist; letter to* Time *magazine, forwarded to Jacqueline Kennedy*

Saturday, November 23, 2:30 A.M.

Dear Sir,

Friday night at 10:30 P.M. (a couple of hours ago and only 1½ hours after the dreadful news of the tragical death of your president which gave us a severe shock), Berlin students initiated a midnight torchlight march by phoning friends and friends and friends of all the various parts of the city. And at midnight in this cold and stormy night ten thousands of students and other Berliners took part in this 1½ hours silent march to honor your hopeful president who is dead now: John F. Kennedy, our all good friend, our all great brother who gave his life for justice and liberty and freedom and tolerance.

Very truly
Yours E. J. Pauw

JFK had also stopped in Frankfurt during his June 1963 visit to Germany. During a speech in the Paulskirche, symbolic site of a democratic Germany because of its association with the revolution of 1848, Kennedy pledged his willingness to put American cities at risk if necessary to defend European freedom.

Berlin motorcade on June 26, 1963. Standing in the car, waving to the crowd, from left to right: President Kennedy, West Berlin Mayor Willy Brandt, and German Chancellor Konrad Adenauer. *JFK Library*

❧ *Werner Bockelmann, High Mayor of Frankfurt-am-Main; typewritten letter*

17th of December 1963
Town Hall-Römerberg

Dear Mrs. Kennedy,

There are few events that are capable of shaking the world and of confronting mankind with its tragic fate. . . .

We in Frankfurt, who have the late President in such lively memory, were stunned when we received the terrible news. . . . At the same time that your husband was carried to his last rest, the population were filing along the streets in pouring rain. . . .

It was a spontaneous mourning, coming straight from the heart, that was gripping the whole town. . . .

The town-council and municipal authorities of Frankfurt have decided to put up a memorial tablet at the "Paulskirche," where your husband delivered his great speech on essential principles and fundamental problems to the Germans. We shall rename a great arterial road, by which your husband left Frankfurt, into "Kennedy-Allee." And we shall keep him in our hearts.

With . . . our deep sympathy and grief,

Werner Bockelmann

The Kennedys' official state visit to Paris in the spring of 1961 was a clear boost to the young leader's prestige on both sides of the Atlantic. His glamorous wife contributed a huge dose of élan to the occasion. Her college year abroad in Paris had been a high point of her youth. Moreover, Jacqueline Kennedy always identified with her father and the French side of her heritage, even if ethnically "Black Jack" Bouvier was more Irish than French. Also, Jackie had felt a lifelong fascination for French President De Gaulle. In fact, more than one family dog had been named for him. When, at the Versailles banquet he was hosting, De Gaulle declared to the First Lady that "You resemble a Watteau," he showed that he knew how to turn a compliment as only a French man could.

❧ *General Charles De Gaulle, President of France, and his wife; telegram, in French*

NOVEMBER 22, 1963
MRS JOHN F KENNEDY
THE IMMENSE GRIEF THAT HAS JUST HIT YOU TOUCHES ME AND MY WIFE IN THE DEEPEST REACHES OF OUR HEARTS BE ASSURED THAT WE ARE BESIDE YOU IN THOUGHT AND PRAYER PRESIDENT KENNEDY WILL NEVER BE FORGOTTEN
GENERAL ET MADAME DE GAULLE

Despite the sometimes prickly chauvinistic pronouncements of De Gaulle, many French leaders favored not only the economic integration of Europe but a more general cooperation with the West. Jean Monnet, a visionary but pragmatic French internationalist, was the guiding spirit behind what became the European Union, and worked for decades with governments around the world promoting economic cooperation. He and his Italian-born wife, Silvia, were personal friends with many of the Western world's leaders.

ও *Silvia Monnet; handwritten letter, in French*

Houjarray

the 25th of November 1963

My dear Mrs. Kennedy,

To tell you the pain we feel from the death of the President feels almost like a selfishly sentimental response when we think how great your sorrow is.

Nevertheless, let me express it, as we felt it with every bit of our heart . . .

Silvia Monnet

In Washington only two weeks after the assassination, Jean Monnet was awarded the Presidential Medal of Freedom (with Special Distinction). At the December 6 ceremony, President Johnson also conferred the Presidential Medal of Freedom posthumously on both Pope John XXIII and President John Fitzgerald Kennedy.

❧ *Jean Monnet; handwritten letter, in French*

The Westchester
Washington, DC
7th December 1963

Dear Mrs. Kennedy—

I was there yesterday among the ones who received the "Presidential Medal of Freedom."

I want to tell you how much I was touched and honored to have been chosen by President Kennedy. . . .

I know the role you played in the presentation and form of this magnificent distinction, the "medal of freedom" and I wanted to thank you—before leaving for Paris. . . .

Jean Monnet

After West Germany and Canada, the nation that generated the largest volume of condolence mail in the aftermath of November 22 was Italy (followed closely by France, and more distantly by the United Kingdom, India, and Ireland). Italy's position may seem surprising until one considers the tremendous popularity and mutual admiration between JFK and John XXIII, the Italian Pope who died in the summer of 1963 and whose forward-looking ecumenicism led to fundamental reforms in the Roman Catholic Church. Also, several Italians numbered among Jackie Kennedy's devoted friends.

☙ *Egidio Ortona, former Italian Ambassador to the United Nations, later Ambassador to the United States; at the time General Director of Economic Affairs, Italian Foreign Ministry; handwritten letter*

12/10/63

Dear Jackie,

Today is the sad meditation of the aftermath, seeing you back into old familiar surroundings, I want to tell you all our great devotion and affection. . . .

We knew your loss was our loss—the loss of a leader whom we had already learned to admire and to consider such, for ourselves and for the whole life of our Atlantic community. . . . Since the old times, when, still a Senator, I decorated him with Italian insignia, to the last time I saw him and he called me, teasingly, "an American," in front of my President—this power of attraction was without limits. . . .

I send you herewith a clipping of an Italian newspaper. . . . You will see how the tragedy of November 22nd was instrumental in bringing about sudden wisdom in my countrymen in a moment of great political crisis. . . .

I hope, Jackie, that you will know how near we are and always will be to you as old devoted admiring friends.

Egidio

The clipping Ortona refers to describes the political compromise reached the day after Kennedy's assassination between Italian Christian Democrats and Socialists that opened the way for the first center-left government since the start of the Cold War.

The social circles Jackie Kennedy moved in when visiting her sister Lee in London were the same as those frequented by the Greek ship-owning tycoons Aristotle Onassis and Stavros Niarchos. Starting in 1961, the two sisters had found diversion and relaxation on cruises aboard Greek yachts, some owned by these two longtime rivals.

🙟 *Eugenia Niarchos, wife of Greek shipping magnate Stavros Niarchos; hand-written letter*

Dear Jackie

I do want to write a few words to tell you of our shock to hear of your great tragedy—and to ask you to accept from both Stavros and myself our . . . deepest sympathy prayers and thoughts. . . . The President was a great man whose death has not only saddened you who knew him and loved him but also everyone else in the world. . . .

With all my thoughts and sympathy.

Eugenie

(Niarchos)

Nov. 29th

Niarchos's enemy, Aristotle Onassis, who came in person to the White House to pay his condolences, was said to entertain both more "flamboyant" jet-setters as well as Arab oilmen of lesser social repute. Although the Greek royal family was thought to be particularly close to Niarchos, Queen Frederica was also known for sometimes frequenting "Ari's" yacht, the *Christina*.

🙟 *King Paul and Queen Frederica of Greece; telegram*

MRS. JACQUELINE KENNEDY—THE WHITE HOUSE—TERRIBLY SHOCKED AND GREATLY MOVED BY THE TERRIBLE NEWS WE DESIRE TO EXPRESS OUR DEEPEST GRIEF AND OUR MOST HEARTFELT SYMPATHY—PAUL R FREDERICA R

Roman Catholics around the world often seemed to feel a special affinity for the young American President. The British peeress Elizabeth Craven wrote from Newbury, Berkshire, "as a fellow Catholic" at whose private home chapel were "offered mass & our prayers last Sunday for your brave husband. . . ." Many women who wrote were associated with the Society of the Sacred Heart, the international Catholic order in which both Rose Fitzgerald and all of her daughters were raised. Mother Mouton and dozens of her students of poetry and rhetoric at the Maison du Sacré Coeur in Ixelles/Brussels, Belgium, wrote a long letter to Mrs. Kennedy expressing admiration for "his ideal . . . to see freedom and peace reign, to lessen anguish around the world."

Cardinal Cicognani, perhaps the most powerful political figure in Vatican City, promised Mrs. Kennedy and her children "copious divine grace of comforting solace" in his telegram, and followed up with a typed letter sent on Christmas Eve. Pope Pius XII, whose death in 1958 had cleared the way for the election of Pope John XXIII, had been a family friend of Jacqueline Kennedy's in-laws, having shared tea with Rose and Joseph Kennedy Sr. in Bronxville when he was still Cardinal Eugenio Pacelli.

᠕ *Prince Carlo Pacelli, nephew to Pope Pius XII; telegram*

VATICAN CITY NOV 23 1963 1120
FAMILY KENNEDY WASHINGTON
PRINCESS PACELLI AND I BEG YOU ACCEPT HEARTFELT
CONDOLENCES AND ASSURANCE OF PRAYERS STOP
OUR LORD HAS CERTAINLY BLESSED AND EMBRACED
PROUD SOUL OF JOHN KENNEDY HEROIC DEFENSOR
DIGNITY AND FREEDOM OF MEN STOP OUR LADY WILL
CONFORM AND ASSIST YOU ALL STOP DEVOTEDLY
YOURS
PRINCE CARLO PACELLI

The common language and personal pre– and post–World War II connections binding the United Kingdom to the Kennedy family ensured a huge outpouring of sympathy and letters from that nation. The British sovereign immediately sent condolences:

➻ *Queen Elizabeth II of the United Kingdom and British Commonwealth; "wet-process" facsimile copy*

I am so deeply distressed to learn of the tragic death of President Kennedy. My husband joins me in sending our heartfelt and sincere sympathy to you and to your family.

Elizabeth R

The Queen Mother, widow of King George VI, also sent a telegram:

```
                          THE WHITE HOUSE
                             WASHINGTON

                       Nov 23  9 17 PM '63

   WN578 40 VIA RCA

                   BUCKINGHAM PALACE LONDON 1220 NOVEMBER 23 1963

   MRS JOHN KENNEDY

              THE WHITE HOUSE WASHINGTON

   I AM SO DEEPLY SHOCKED AND GRIEVED TO HEAR OF THE DEATH

   OF PRESIDENT KENNEDY MY THOUGHTS AND PRAYERS ARE MUCH WITH

   YOU IN THIS MOMENT OF GREAT SORROW

        ELIZABETH R QUEEN MOTHER
```

William Manchester provides a report in his *Death of a President* of "London teenagers . . . just distraught, openly crying in the streets." Former British Prime Minister Anthony Eden and his wife called the death of Kennedy "the most grievous blow of this century." Labour Party leader and future Prime Minister Harold Wilson not only sent Mrs. Kennedy a letter of solace and admiration, but turned up at the funeral—this after what Manchester calls "a giddy moment [when] it appeared that both houses of Parliament were on their way" to the ceremonies as well. John Masefield, British Poet Laureate to the Court, wrote a prayerful verse that was widely disseminated as a black-edged mourning card.

The President of Cyprus, Archbishop Makarios, had known Kennedy as a Senator and was also welcomed officially at the White House. In an Oral History statement prepared later for the JFK Library, he suggested this epitaph for JFK, from the Greek poet Pindar:

> *O Megas, I cannot bring you back to life:*
> *Only despair awaits those who would attempt the feat.*
> *Now I raise up in your city*
> *This marble column of the Muses in order to honor*
> *The day when you ran races . . .*

Not all reactions from Western Europe were pure messages of solace, however; some felt that the violence raised deep concern about the nature of American society itself. For example, one eighteen-year-old Swedish engineering student who had just spent a summer in the United States pointed out that the double murders of the preceding days had hurt "Americans' reputation very much. I wonder if you can ever repair it."

Jack Kennedy had been so entranced by his brief visit to Ireland in June that he played and replayed movies of the trip until only the diehard would keep him company. He visited his distant cousin Mary Kennedy Ryan in the ancestral Kennedy village of Dunganstown in County Wexford—his only visit since going there with sister Kathleen in 1947—and was the first foreign head of state to address the Irish Parliament. Back home, he played with the idea of becoming Ambassador to Ireland after the presidency, and in Limerick he used the words of a song to promise to come "back with the Shamrock in the Springtime."

ᔐ *Eamon De Valera, president of Ireland; telegram*

DUBLIN IRISH GOVERNMENT 70 22 2200
MRS JOHN F KENNEDY
THE WHOLE IRISH PEOPLE MOURN IN SYMPATHY
WITH YOU . . . AND WE PRAY THAT THE SOUL OF
YOUR HUSBAND WHO HAD BECOME SO DEAR TO US
HERE MAY NOW BE WITH GOD IN HEAVEN . . .
EAMON DE VALERA

After visiting the Kennedy side of his family in Dunganstown, Kennedy had stopped at the Loreto Convent in Wexford to visit a cousin on his mother's side.

ᔐ *Mother Superior M. J. Clement (Flossie Fitzgerald Ward); handwritten letter and photograph*

My dear Mrs. Kennedy,

I want to convey to you on behalf of myself, the community and the pupils our very sincere and heartfelt sympathy. . . . If we, who met him only for a few short moments, have been so numbed by the awful tragedy I cannot dare to think of how you must feel. . . .

I am glad he had visited Ireland. It gave him great pleasure and we took him entirely to our hearts and looked on him as our own. We were already looking forward to seeing him again "in the Spring." The visit reaped for him a great spiritual harvest. I think I am safe in saying that there is nobody, of any Creed, in the country who has not mourned his loss and prayed for the repose of his soul and for you. . . .

Yours very sincerely in J.C.,

M. J. Clement (Fitzgerald)

Back in Dublin, he had seen many Irish political figures, including Declan Costello, a member of the lower house, and his father, John Costello, the former Taoiseach, or prime minister. At dinner with Costello and President De Valera the last night of his trip the group had a lively talk about the qualities of different Irish fighting songs.

❧ *Declan Costello, member of the Irish Dail and future High Court judge; handwritten letter*

Dublin

24/11/63

My dear Jacqueline,

. . . For Joan & me, the President's death has been like a death in our own family. . . . We have remembered your visit to our home with great affection and, since then, have followed your triumphs, and your trials, with a personal concern—suffering, and rejoicing with you. We now mourn with you, deeply, sincerely, wholeheartedly . . .

All over the world there are people like me, engaged in the public affairs of our own countries, for whom the President's great moral stature has been a source of inspiration and guidance. His death will not change this—rather, it will enhance it. . . .

Father Leonard, whom I visited yesterday, was deeply grieved. He told my father that he had felt nothing so deeply since his mother's death fifty years ago. . . .

Very sincerely yours,
Declan Costello
5th December 1963

The Father Leonard referred to above was a priest at a well-known college in Dublin that prepared students for the priesthood. Jack renewed their acquaintance on this trip, but it was Jackie who on a trip in 1950 had first made contact with this old friend of the Bouvier family.

❧ *Father Leonard, professor at All Hallow College, Dublin; handwritten letter*

1 December 1963

My dearest Jacqueline,

I shall not write to write a letter of sympathy. I could not find the words. Instead, I shall ask you to do me a favour, and that is, to let me unite my simple feelings of love, grief and desolation to your profound and heartfelt ones.

I think the President promoted and defended principles in favour of the rights of the poor, the neglected and the outcast, and as these are Christian principles and as he died in defence of them, he is a Christian martyr. I think that you have given the women, not only of the USA but of the world, a representation of the ideal of the Valiant Woman as she appeared in the eyes of Solomon. . . . I have not been well for some time and so unable to say Mass since last Christmas Day. I wrote to Rome for permission to celebrate it sitting down. Strange to say the permission arrived on the day and almost at the hour the President died, so that I had the consolation of saying Mass for the repose of his soul on Sunday 24th. The next mass will be for January 1 & the children.

I was so pleased to learn that Father Huber, the priest who gave him the last sacraments is a Vincentian, the Order to which I belong. Our friendship has been one of the greatest blessings & happiness of my life.

Love as ever

Father Leonard

President Kennedy remained as committed to Israeli security as Truman and Eisenhower, and Israel's influential Foreign Minister Golda Meir attended the funeral, along with Israel's largely ceremonial president (Prime Minister Ben Gurion had stepped down in June of the same year). The most important aspect of JFK's Middle East policy, however—beyond, perhaps, trying to convince the Shah of Iran to democratize his society— was the opening of a serious dialogue with Gamal Abdel Nasser. Nasser was a pan-Arab nationalist and President of Egypt—then still officially called the United Arab Republic, even though its union with Syria had dissolved two years earlier.

𝕫❧ *Gamal Abdel Nasser, President of Egypt; telegram, in French*

HELIOPOLIS, CAIRO NOVEMBER 22 1963
MADAME JACQUELINE KENNEDY
THE PEOPLE OF THE UNITED ARAB REPUBLIC AND I
MYSELF ARE PROFOUNDLY SHOCKED BY THIS UN-
SPEAKABLE CRIME OF WHICH YOUR VERY REGRETTED
AND VERY ILLUSTRIOUS HUSBAND IS A VICTIM AT THE
MOMENT WHEN FULL OF YOUTH AND HOPE AND
VIGOR HE FOUGHT FOR HIS PEOPLE AND FOR HUMAN-
ITY WE ALL SHARE THE SORROW WITH WHICH YOU
LIVE THIS PAINFUL DRAMA I AM CONVINCED THAT
THE LOSS EXPERIENCED BY THE FORCES FOR PEACE

AND PROGRESS IN THE WORLD IS NO LESS THAN THAT
FELT BY THE AMERICAN PEOPLE AND YOURSELF . . .
GAMAL ABDEL NASSER

Though it's hard to fathom now given their divergent historical reputations, Kennedy valued highly his rapport with the then forty-four-year-old Shah of Iran, Mohamed Pahlavi. Pahlavi and his glamorous twenty-five-year-old wife, Farah Diba, sometimes rivaled Jack and Jackie in the amount of press coverage they generated for jet-set gossip columns. The Shah declared in his telegram that "this dastardly act . . . deprived the world of one of its most esteemed and distinguished leaders, while his wife wrote a personal note:

☙ *Empress Farah Pahlavi of Iran; handwritten letter in French*

> 23 November 1963
> Tehran

Dear Madame Kennedy

   With all my heart I am with you to share your so profound sorrow. . . .

   I did not want to believe such a thing, such a thing could not be true! These few words are really so poor for expressing what I feel in this sad mourning.

   We weep for a great friend, as the world does a Great Man.

> Very affectionately
> Farah

If the famous soirées at the Kennedy White House represented the symbolic triumph of a Hemingway/Fitzgerald–style "moveable feast," they were also the first state-sanctioned social events to break through long-standing racial and colonial barriers. The world was changing, especially on the other side of the Mediterranean from where Jackie and Lee began their cruises. Since his days as a senator, JFK had been a champion of Algerian independence and of emerging nations in Africa and Asia, often to the displeasure of the Eisenhower administration. Neophyte leaders of the scores of African countries that had just or were just about to gain independence were greeted warmly at Kennedy's White House.

Among the heads of state who had grown close to both Kennedys during JFK's years in office was Ethiopian Emperor Haile Selassie. Though he was eventually deposed and died in prison, the Emperor had a populist appeal among his own people, enjoyed a history of support among African-Americans in the United States, and had led troops against the Italians during World War II. He is regarded to this day as a divine being by the Rastafarian religious movement (which derives its name from the Emperor's given name Tafari). Selassie and his granddaughter Ruth had paid a state visit to Washington only a month before the assassination; in the funeral procession on November 25 he took pride of place next to General de Gaulle.

❧ *Emperor Haile Selassie of Ethiopia; telegram*

ADDIS ABABA
WORDS ARE INADEQUATE TO EXPRESS THE GRIEF AND SHOCK WHICH WE FEEL AT THE TRAGIC DEATH OF YOUR HUSBAND AND OUR GOOD FRIEND . . . HIS DEVOTION TO THE SERVICE OF MANKIND HAS EARNED FOR HIM AN ENDURING PLACE IN THE HEARTS AND AFFECTION OF MEN EVERYWHERE STOP WE RECALL OUR MEETING WITH YOU BOTH IN WASHINGTON ONLY A FEW SHORT WEEKS AGO . . . IN THIS TIME OF

PAIN AND SUFFERING WE . . . PRAY THAT ALMIGHTY
GOD WILL LEND YOU SUPPORT AND SUCCOUR . . .
HAILE SELASSIE 1ST EMPEROR

Kennedy was also not hesitant about toasting the North African Arabs who
had fought and sacrificed for their independence from European powers.
Both Jack and Jackie were particularly close to the Moroccan royal family.
Ahmed Ben Bella, first President of an independent Algeria and a close ally
of Egypt's Nasser, came to the White House as a luncheon guest in October
1962. And at the very first White House dinner for a chief of state, held on
May 3, 1961, President Kennedy saluted President Habib Bourguiba of Tunisia for spending many months in prison while struggling for his country's
independence. In fact, his son Habib Bourguiba Jr.—who served as Tunisia's
Ambassador in Washington not only during Kennedy's presidency but during part of Eisenhower's—is sometimes given credit for influencing then
Senator Kennedy's 1957 declaration in favor of Algerian independence from
France.

❧ *Moufida Bourguiba, wife of the President of Tunisia and mother of the*
Tunisian Ambassador to the United States; handwritten letter in French

Tunis the 25 November 1963

Madame,

I am devastated by this sad news. . . . I was very happy and very proud
of the friendly relations my son enjoyed with your so valorous husband.
We know . . . what a loss it is for you and your two small children . . .
but also for the poor and colored people. His bright and generous politics
recognized by the entire world. . . . How pleased I was by the friendly
feelings my son and his young wife had towards you when they were at

the Embassy! . . . You will have many beautiful things to tell Caroline and John Jr. about the life of their papa. . . . Courage to you then, Madame, who have known so young how to be a Great Lady. . . .

Moufida Bourguiba,
Mother of M. Habib Bourguiba Jr.

The new leaders of Francophone sub-Saharan Africa also found themselves courted by the young American President, who hoped to provide them with other interlocutors than their French "mentors." One of JFK's favorites was Félix Houphouet-Boigny from the Ivory Coast and his wife. Another with whom JFK exchanged mutual respect was Senegal's first president, Léopold Sédar Senghor—a poet politician and intellectual who as a student in Paris in the 1930s had co-invented the influential Négritude movement. In a follow-up letter in early February 1964, Senghor wrote Jacqueline Kennedy, in French, that he had read Kennedy's writings and "considered him one of the most important figures of Modern History."

The new and not-yet-born nations of Anglophone Black Africa mourned JFK with perhaps an even greater passion than those of North Africa and Senegal. Like many others, Nigerian president Nnamdi Azikiwe compared the late President to Lincoln; "Zik," as he was known, was a great admirer of the American educational system and had requested a large number of Peace Corps volunteers as teachers. Crispin Olu Martins and Peter A. Omoworare, respectively secretary and president of the new Kennedy Youth Club of Nigeria, for whom John F. Kennedy had been "a ministering angel to the whole world," talked in their letter to the First Lady about JFK's "noble inspirations" and "his great and living deeds of peace, love and unity." Jomo Kenyatta, the Kenyan leader once imprisoned by the British who would become the new country's first president three weeks after JFK's assassination, wired Mrs. Kennedy that the tragedy was a "great loss for Africa." Also wiring sympathy was the last Arab Sultan of

Zanzibar—a leader who would be overthrown some six weeks later. Thereafter the country would merge with Tanganyika to become the amalgamated state of Tanzania, under the leadership of Julius Nyerere.

🐾 *Julius Nyerere, President of Tanganyika; typewritten letter*

> The State House
> Dar Es Salaam
> Tanganyika
> 22nd November 1963

Dear Mrs. Kennedy,

There is nothing which I or anyone can say to console you or express the loss which your husband's death brings.

As President of Tanganyika I mourn for the death of one of the greatest Presidents of the United States, whose efforts for peace have been a major factor in the recent easing of international tension. But in the midst of my deep consciousness of our loss in the national leader, I remember the man. In doing so I know something of our trouble now. May God help you to bear this great suffering.

> Yours sincerely,
> Julius K. Nyerere

In Latin America in the fall of 1963, military coups in the Dominican Republic (September) and Ecuador (October) signaled the rough road ahead for many of the progressive, reformist aspirations of Kennedy's Alliance for Progress. At least one of the Alliance's key supporters, however— Venezuelan President Rómulo Betancourt—retained his political strength. Part of his popularity derived from having survived a 1960 attempt on his life organized by Dominican dictator Rafael Trujillo (himself assassinated by fellow countrymen not long afterward).

‌❧ *Rómulo Betancourt, President of Venezuela; telegram in Spanish*

CARACAS 1550 NOVEMBER 22 1963
MRS. KENNEDY
A COMPASSIONATE AND AFFECTIONATE EMBRACE TO
YOU AND A KISS AND BENEDICTION TO YOUR CHIL-
DREN (STOP) I AM WITH YOU WITH ALL MY HEART
FROM SUCH HIGH REGARD FOR YOUR HUSBAND JOHN
OF WHOM I SHALL ALWAYS PRESERVE THE MEMORY OF
A GREAT FRIEND EMBRACES
ROMULO BETANCOURT PRESIDENT OF VENEZUELA

Eusebio Dávalos Hurtado, director of the Museum of Anthropology in
Mexico City, recalled in his letter to Mrs. Kennedy the honor of having
escorted the First Couple through his exhibits during their visit in June of
1962. The left-leaning President of Brazil, João Goulart, who would himself
be overthrown by a military coup in little more than four months, sent a
telegram in Portuguese expressing the deep sorrow shared by all Brazil-
ians. The conservative President of Chile, Jorge Alessandri, who had found
himself pushed to the left by events in Cuba and Kennedy's own Alliance
for Progress, spoke nonetheless of the "many displays of friendship offered
my government and myself." Respectable sources have claimed that Haiti's
dictator Papa Doc Duvalier boasted that Kennedy had been killed because of a curse Duvalier had leveled at him, but on November 22 he sent
a carefully worded telegram of sympathy to Jacqueline Kennedy.

Wherever Jacqueline Kennedy traveled, she left a vivid memory. Those
who had had the honor of guiding or escorting her on her visits abroad
sent personal, often heartfelt condolence telegrams and letters. Among

these were Bashir Ahmed, the policeman and "camel driver" who "had the great honour of escorting you in Karachi" on her spring 1962 visit to Pakistan, and Mohammed Ahmad Kahn from Agra, India, "your guide on your last visit to the Taj Mahal."

Although Kennedy's personal relationship with India's Prime Minister Jawaharlal Nehru was never warm, American ties to India strengthened considerably while Kennedy's close political adviser John Kenneth Galbraith served as U.S. Ambassador in New Delhi. Nehru's daughter, who became India's first (and still only) female prime minister in 1966, both visited Washington and played hostess to Jacqueline Kennedy during the First Lady's South Asia tour. In a typewritten letter sent from the Prime Minister's House, Indira Gandhi wondered "if there is another instance in history when a single individual has so symbolised the hopes and aspirations of . . . people spread all over the world," and praised "the warmth and essential humaneness" of President Kennedy.

During her stay in India Mrs. Kennedy also made a stop in Udaipur, Mewar—a princely kingdom incorporated into India under the 1947 constitution.

Bhagwat Singhji, Maharana of Mewar; typewritten letter

The Palace
Udaipur
Mewar
30th November, 1963

My dear Jacqueline Kennedy,

The shocking news of Mr. Kennedy's assassination literally stunned us. Only a fanatic or a lunatic could act in this manner towards a man proceeding for a humane service.

The world is deprived of a great man and a noble soul. . . .

Whenever you should travel towards this part of the world, . . . you are always welcome to Udaipur.

With kindest regards and love,

Sincerely yours

Bhagwat

Perhaps the most famous of the Kennedys' official functions was the July 1961 state dinner held on the grounds of Mount Vernon in honor of Pakistan's President Ayub Khan. One of Pakistan's senior diplomats wrote Mrs. Kennedy from New York:

᳚ *Syed Amjad Ali, former Pakistani Ambassador to the United States, soon-to-be Pakistan's Ambassador to the United Nations; typewritten letter*

Pakistan Mission to the United States

29th November 1963

Dear Mrs. Kennedy,

. . . What you have lost, few women in history have and how you have endured it there are still fewer in history. . . .

The death of Socrates, the martyrdom of Hussain, the murder of Hamlet and the assassination of Lincoln were great losses, but were they only losses? Freedom of thought, righteousness of rulers, exposure of treachery and equality of man were concepts worth the laying down of lives. The last and recent tragic loss likewise reasserts those great concepts which call for a supreme sacrifice. That sacrifice was made. Let us hope we are worthy of it.

Sincerely,

Syed Amjad Ali

Two heads of state were assassinated in November 1963. The military coup that resulted in the assassination on November 1 of South Vietnam's President Ngo Dinh Diem had been sanctioned by Kennedy himself in a moment of confusion and frustration—a decision he sorely regretted. For months preceding that coup, the government of President Diem had been without official representation in Washington, and after November 1, the Vietnamese Embassy staff was in turmoil. So the diplomat sending condolences to Mrs. Kennedy was only an "interim" appointee:

☙ *Pham Khac Rau, interim chargé d'affaires at the South Vietnamese Embassy in Washington; handwritten letter*

> Embassy of Viet Nam
> Washington DC
> November twenty-second, 1963

Dear Mrs. Kennedy,

It is with great shock and deep regrets that we learned of the passing of the President.

You have our deepest sympathy and with the world we mourn the cruelty of your loss—

> Very sincerely,
> Pham Khac Rau
> Chargé d'affaires a.i.

The former South Vietnamese Ambassador to Washington, Than Trai Tran Van Chuong, was also the estranged father of Madame Ngo Dinh Nhu and in-law of Ngo Dinh Diem. On November 25 he wrote to Mrs. Kennedy: "Indeed, fate is incomprehensibly unjust and cruel."

Not all nations or leaders in the world actively mourned for the martyred President in the days after November 22. Early in his 1960 campaign Kennedy had expressed fleeting interest in recognizing Communist China. As President, he quickly concluded it made more sense to isolate it, and the People's Republic responded with open hostility. Meanwhile, Taiwan, or Nationalist China, remained suspicious of Kennedy's intentions. Its President, Chiang Kai-shek, sent a diplomatically correct condolence telegram (as did other officials), but it was one of the few allies not to send a special delegation to the funeral.

❧ *Chiang Kai-shek, President of the Republic of China; telegram*

TAIPEI 42 23 1232P
MRS. JOHN F KENNEDY
MADAME CHIANG AND I ARE SHOCKED AND GRIEVED
TO LEARN OF THE TRAGIC DEATH OF PRESIDENT JOHN
F KENNEDY STOP PLEASE ACCEPT OUR HEARTFELT
SYMPATHY AND CONDOLENCES IN YOUR BEREAVE-
MENT
CHIANG KAI-SHEK

Perhaps in response to raised eyebrows at Taiwan's absence of representation at the funeral, Madame Chiang Kai-shek wrote a separate condolence letter to Ambassador Joseph Kennedy in late January. In it, she defended as farsighted her and her husband's "cries in the wilderness" against "human degradation" (perpetrated by the Communists).

Almost cataclysmic at the start of Kennedy's administration, relations between the United States and the Soviet Union had warmed considerably by the time he died. Ilya Ehrenburg, for decades one of the most visible and adaptable of Soviet journalist/intellectuals, wrote in a wire to

Hubert Humphrey, which the Senator promised to pass on to Mrs. Kennedy, that the President had been a "noble and peace-loving man" and "only a villain could assassinate such a man." Nothing, however, could have been more significant for the fate of both countries than the genuine distress and sorrow felt in both the Kremlin and on the streets of the Soviet Union.

Nikita Khrushchev, Premier and First Secretary of the Communist Party of the Soviet Union; telegram, in Russian

WN150 70 VIA RCA
MOSCOW 1215 NOVEMBER 23 1963
MRS. JACQUELINE KENNEDY
WITH DEEP PERSONAL SORROW I LEARNED ABOUT THE TRAGIC DEATH OF YOUR HUSBAND—THE PRESIDENT OF USA JOHN F. KENNEDY. IN EVERYONE WHO KNEW HIM HE INSPIRED GREAT RESPECT, AND MY MEETINGS WITH HIM WILL FOREVER REMAIN IN MY MEMORY. PLEASE ACCEPT MY MOST SINCERE CONDOLENCES AND EXPRESSIONS OF MY DEEPEST SYMPATHY ON THE DEEP SORROW THAT BEFELL YOU.
N. KHRUSHCHEV
23 OF NOVEMBER 1963

Jacqueline Kennedy understood perfectly the import of this telegram, and did not hesitate to carefully compose a reply, itself reviewed by the U.S. State Department, in which she praised Khrushchev as a "big man" who—unlike the little ones moved by "fear and pride"—was a partner with her husband "in a determination that the world should not be blown up." The day after Christmas, Nina Khrushcheva, the premier's wife, sent a New

Наилучшие пожелания
в Новом году!

My best wishes to you
and your family
in the New Year.

Nina Khrushcheva

26/XII - 1963.
Moscow.

From Nina Khrushcheva, the wife of the Soviet premier.

Year's card from Moscow offering her "best wishes," which was personally sent on to Mrs. Kennedy by the Soviet Ambassador, Anatoly Dobrynin.

Yugoslavia's importance as a possible breakaway from the Communist bloc had been highlighted by President Kennedy's appointment of veteran Cold War strategist George F. Kennan as Ambassador to Belgrade. Frustrations and misunderstandings had so multiplied, however—some as the result of Congressional bullheadedness—that Kennan had left his post the previous July, leaving no ambassadorial representation at the time of the assassination. Nonetheless, strongman Josip Broz Tito sent a long telegram characterizing President Kennedy's "life and work" as "indispensable not only for the American people but for the community of nations as well." Meanwhile, the "dilapidated" Consulate General building in the Croatian city of Zagreb was suddenly brightened by a great quantity of flowers brought in "an obviously spontaneous display of sincere grief," according to U.S. diplomats there.

Poland was another Communist country particularly sympathetic to Kennedy, perhaps because it was strongly Catholic. John Cabot, the seasoned ambassador stationed in Warsaw, also had responsibility for maintaining, through the embassy, the only regular United States contact with China. In a warm personal note sent to Mrs. Kennedy shortly before Christmas, his wife, Lyanth, called the preceding weeks "a month of sadness" in which, "under the watchful eyes of the police," many thousands of Poles came to the Embassy to sign the official condolence book, leaving behind flowers, toys for Caroline and John-John, and other tokens. Direct eyewitnesses to the outpouring in Warsaw were Nobel- and Pulitzer Prize–winning author John Steinbeck and his wife, Elaine, sent on a cultural mission to Iron Curtain countries by President Kennedy. In a handwritten letter sent from Warsaw dated November 24, 1963, Steinbeck also described the seemingly endless line of ordinary citizens who filed through the embassy all day and all night, many of them weeping. He wrote that he "had never seen anything like this respect and this reverence."

One of the reverential Poles who sent a letter to Ambassador Cabot was a young boy. He and his five brothers (there would be six by 1964) hoped to ease Caroline and John-John's distress by having them visit.

◆ *Boleslaw "Bolek" Rey, twelve-year-old boy; handwritten letter in Polish*

Please Sir,

The news that Mr. President has been murdered is awful. Why didn't his soldiers know how to guard him better? My Mom and Dad and everybody are very upset. I am also very upset because I read and hear everywhere what a good man he was. Poor Mrs. President. I am very sorry for their children who must be crying for their Daddy. Please tell them not to cry because I am praying with the little ones for the soul of Mr. President.

Or Sir, bring them to us here. We will play with them so that they will be less sad. We are learning English so we will somehow understand each other. Janek knows English better than I but he is in a sanatorium now. But he will be back for Christmas and we will have two weeks off from school so let them come then. We will do so that they do not cry, and there are five of us, so everyone will always think of something amusing for them. Wladek and Jozek are actually still too young, but Janek, me and Jurek are not. I am so sorry about Mr. President. On photographs he was always smiling and happy. Please tell them everything I have written here.

Bolek Rey

W-wa 23 XI 63 r.

Pan Ambasador U.S.A.

Proszę Pana.

Ta wiadomość że zamordowano Pana Prezydenta jest straszna. Czemu jego żołnierze

. . .

On zawsze taki wesoły i uśmiechnięty był na fotografiach. Niech im Pan powie to wszystko co tu napisałem.

Dowidzenia Panu

Bolek Rey.

Eight

VOICES OF THE YOUNG

It seems to me . . . that the essence of the American mood this very dark weekend is this deep feeling that our youth has been mocked, and the vigor of America for the moment paralyzed. . . .
—ALISTAIR COOKE, NOVEMBER 24, 1963

*P*resident Kennedy held a special affinity for young people everywhere. The very premise of his 1960 campaign had been the need to inject energy, vigor, and idealism into what he saw as a complacent consumer society—to "get the country moving again." Before he was elected, the dominant mood among young people was often described as apathetic and self-interested, even alienated. JFK's direct appeal to young people's higher aspirations caught a cultural wave that seemed to be growing all around the world and would crest later in the decade.

Equally important, children were an integral part of daily life at the White House. It was not just Caroline and John-John's occasional visits to the Oval Office, or that they were introduced to every official visitor as part of the routine. Caroline also went to school five days a week in the solarium on the top floor of the White House. The school of a dozen or so kids, mostly children of friends and associates, had its own special performances and parent visitation days. An ongoing series of music programs for young people featured performances by youth orchestras, choruses, and dancers, and brought onto the White House grounds diverse groups of older children as an audience. No wonder social secretary Letitia Baldrige declared,

John Jr. salutes in his new sailor's outfit, a birthday gift that he had just received at his and Caroline's joint birthday party on December 4, 1963, shortly before the family left the White House forever.
Robert L. Knudsen, White House/JFK Library

"We seemed to be entertaining young people constantly."

Many of the condolence letters make clear the extraordinary kinship young children felt for Caroline and John-John, even though they were complete strangers. In Lakewood, California, Mrs. Nancy Higuera's three-and-a-half-year-old daughter acted as if she was personally acquainted with them and refused to comprehend her mother's explanations as to why she too couldn't go to "Caroline's school" in the White House. From California, Ava Jean Talamontez, a nine-year-old transfixed by the horses in the funeral procession, wrote the First Lady that "it's too bad Caroline won't have her daddy to ride with her, but he will always be riding the black horse."

᷿ *Danny Spitsnogle from Odell, Nebraska; handwritten letter*

Dear Caroline,

I am sorry to hear about your Daddy. God will take good care of him. I am ten years old. I am in the fourth grade. I have two pets. My daddy drives the school bus and I ride on it. We live on a farm. I have a pet chicken. She is all black. She is six years old. We have cows too. I like to play football. We went past your grandfather's place in Palm Beach several years ago. I saw you playing outside.

Your friend,
Danny Spitsnogle

Through late November and December of 1963 gifts and offerings, including many from children, piled up in the offices next to the White House where volunteers were sorting Mrs. Kennedy's condolence mail. Lokie and Chrissy Van Roijen, kids who raised bunnies across the street in Georgetown, wrote to Caroline and John Jr., offering each a white rabbit: "baby ones or full grown." A young girl from Chicago named Debbie Cowley wrote Mrs. Kennedy, providing her home address and requesting that the First Lady and her kids come visit since her mother had said her own family couldn't afford the trip to Washington. If that was out of the question, maybe at least they could become pen pals? And a young girl from the Midwest made sure to add a concretely sweet touch to the sympathy letter she sent Mrs. Kennedy after reading the photographic memorial put out by the Associated Press:

ᔆ *Mary Hall, from Racine, Wisconsin; handwritten letter*

Dear Mrs. Kennedy

I saw your Picture in *The Torch Is Passed* it was very pretty and your husband was very nice.

My class and I prayed for him

Our family prays for you and your family

Since Mr. Kennedy was gone things don't seem right. I hope you are happy

Mary Hall age 7
here is some candy

Public and parochial school classes, scout troops, 4-H clubs, sports teams, gym classes, and civic organizations of young people sent group tributes, usually under the guiding hand of an adult leader. There was, for example, a Happy Blue Bird Troop from the Maricopa County Council of Girl Scouts in Phoenix, Arizona; or the following class from Puerto Rico:

❧ *Second-graders from Mayagüez, Puerto Rico; handwritten letter*

> November 26, 1963
>
> Dear John Jr. and Caroline:
> We feel very much the death of your father. We feel unhappy.
>
> > Your friends of
> > second grade of
> > the Manuel Fernandez
> > Juneas School

Older children often composed their own rituals honoring the President:

❧ *Linda Christison, from Dunsmuir, California; handwritten letter*

> November 22, 1963
>
> Dear Mrs. Kennedy,
>   I am sending you this tribute which I made up during my lunch hour at school. It is in my own words, although I know all Americans and all the people of the world feel the same.
>   I sincerely hope from this tribute you may find some condolence
>
> > Respectfully yours,
> > Linda Christison
> > 6th grade

President Kennedy

1st person: We would like to pay a special tribute to President Kennedy.

2nd person: President Kennedy fought for his convictions, for this we are proud.

3rd person: President Kennedy fought for everybody regardless of color or race so they too, could have equal rights, for this we are proud.

2nd person: President Kennedy worked for world peace, this demonstrated by the test ban treaty, for this we are proud.

3rd person: President Kennedy believed in helping other countries by giving aid, for this we are proud.

1st person: President Kennedy believed in the United States' power and showed it during the Cuban Crisis, for this we are proud.

1st person: We are all proud of this great man.

Linda Christison

❧ *The Sweet Tarts, from Davey, Nebraska, handwritten card and letter*

Davey, Nebraska
Dec. 6, 1963

Dear Mrs. Kennedy,

We were all deeply touched when we heard about the death of the President. On December 5, 1963 the club called "Sweet Tarts" held a small dedication for your husband. That drastic, unbelievable day, we all decided to write some dedications for your husband. The President of our club will take these dedications and place them in a box and place it in a sacred part of her room. The box, along side of his picture, will never be opened again.

The flag that we used in our dedication service we now present to you.

With our sympathy we hope you and yours will stand head held high.

Lovingly,
"The Sweet-Tarts"

Anniversaries and birthdays became touchstones for repeated acts of mourning and devotion. Shortly before what would have been John F. Kennedy's forty-seventh birthday on May 29, 1964, a group of unrelated girls from Union, New Jersey, all sent individual letters of sympathy and remembrance. In Ohio, Susan Lee Guggenheim, a twelve-year-old girl who was particularly enamored of the way Mrs. Kennedy had decorated the White House, spoke for many other girls her age in declaring that "when I grow up I wish to become like you, courageous, valiant, majestic, marvelous, and most of all beautiful."

Some young people took the news so much to heart it led to an emotional catharsis. Linda Pilas from Illinois made an altar in her room with her autographed souvenir photo of JFK and "cried and cried until I was purple"; she loved the First Lady and President "more than ever," she affirmed in her letter. Deborah Annette Mizelle, a twelve-year-old girl from Richmond Heights, Florida, who had sent President Kennedy a picture of herself some years earlier, asked that Mrs. Kennedy place the picture close to the dead president "on his heart. If it is too late put it in a hole on top of his grave." And in one instance that approached real trauma, a girl from Illinois wrote Mrs. Kennedy that she had "become limp," "began crying and somehow did not know how to stop." She had not been able to sleep since Friday afternoon the twenty-second, and really believed she "was dying." Now, a week later, she "felt the same way." If she didn't get a reply from the First Lady, she "didn't know what she was going to do."

At least one attempt made by a group of children to commemorate the President's death resulted in personal injury. In Memphis, a nine-year-old boy, Lynn Reynolds, his brothers, and friends decided to hold a memorial "moaning" for the President in a ramshackle hut near his home. They got a candle burning on a broken table, lit sparklers purchased from their own hard-earned funds, and made torches out of rags and sticks and paint thinner. When the paint thinner spilled over the candle, an explosion of flame inflicted terrible burns on young Lynn. Luckily, after a brush with pneumonia and weeks of plastic surgery, the young boy was on the road to recovery, according to St. Joseph Hospital Chaplain Rev. Colman Borgard, who in late January wrote to Jacqueline Kennedy about the scars engendered by the boy's noble intentions.

Spontaneous candor and surprising associations were common in the reactions gathered from very young children by sisters from Our Lady of Lourdes Convent Kindergarten in Chicago: "I'm glad the soldiers marched so well. . . . I hate that bad gun. . . . Men let Mrs. Kennedy and children peek at Daddy. . . . I'll see Kennedy when I die, right sister? . . . I'm glad my name is Jacqueline. . . . I hope I'll marry a Mr. President. . . . I prayed for Kennedy under the blanket."

Besides being uncensored, some young children expressed surprisingly adult concerns in their letters to Mrs. Kennedy. Third-grader Lowell Miron of Brooklyn, for example, hoped "you have enough money to support you and your children." Carola Ann Kieve, a nine-year-old girl from Santa Fe, New Mexico, wrote Mrs. Kennedy: "I bet you have a lot of letters to read!" Young David Mezzolo from Chicago thought the late President "was a very brave man to fight Cuba and stick up for his, yours, and our, lives." In a perhaps less idealistic vein, nine-year-old Kenneth Purcell from Stony Brook, Long Island, declared his affection for the late President by pledging to buy a PT-109 as soon as his neighborhood store got in its next order.

2❧ *Richard Thau; handwritten letter*

Nov 22, 1963

Dear Mrs Kennedy
    I hope you don't feel bad
    I feel bad too
    PresIdent Lincoln and
    PresIdent McKinLey and

PresIdent Kennedy,
those PresIdents were
killed. Kiss your Children.
Richard Thau
7 years old
I Live at Kew Gardens. N.Y. New York

❧ *Matthew Gamser, young boy from Washington, D.C.; handwritten letter*

Nov. 22, 1963

Dear Mrs. Kennedy, John Jr. and Caroline,

I wished that your husband did not die.

My father worked for him.

He will be at the white house tomorrow.

I know how sad you must feel.

I feel just as sad as you.

I hope the man that shot him won't shoot President Lyndon Johnson if he goes to Dallas.

Love Matthew S. Gamser

❧ *Kate Pond; handwritten letter*

A Friend

Woodside CA

Dear Mrs. Kennedy,

I am only 9 1/2, but I nearly cried when I heard the shocking news. My little sister, Liz, was screaming, "My President, my President."

JFK in the Oval Office clapping while Caroline and John Jr. cavort, October 10, 1962.
Cecil Stoughton, White House/JFK Library

He was such a *good* man and maybe the Good Lord thought he would be nice to have around at an early age, so he took him. If you want to send a letter to the President, send it to

care of the Good Lord . . .
President John F. Kennedy
House of the Presidents Heaven

Send it by air mail.
Keep this in mind.

Yours truly,
A sympathetic friend
Kate Pond

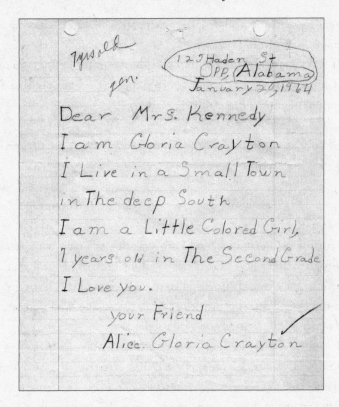

2❧ *Alice Gloria Crayton; handwritten letter*

Opp, Alabama
January 20, 1964

Dear Mrs. Kennedy

I am Gloria Crayton. I Live in a Small Town in The deep South. I am
a Little Colored Girl, 7 years old in The Second Grade. I Love you.

your Friend
Alice Gloria Crayton

For some more mature children, the assassination awakened suddenly adult sensations. Kenneth L. Weir, a sixth-grader from Paducah, Kentucky, who talked about himself as "a child" but in "this case" with "feelings of a man," found himself "for the first time . . . truthfully . . . able to say that I am ashamed to be an American."

ℰ❧ *Chuck Slick, seventh-grader at the Lovett School, Atlanta; handwritten letter*

Atlanta, Georgia
November 27, 1963

Dear Mrs. Kennedy,

My name is Chuck Slick, and I am sure that you have never heard of me. But naturally I have heard of you and my heart goes out to you.

I think that a tragedy has befallen the country and the free world. For when the United States of America loses a leader, the West and aspiring free Nations of the East receive a dire setback.

Having been born in Texas, I felt nauseated when I was told of this frightening blow. It makes me angry at Dallas, even though my half-brother lives there.

Also I must say that I admire your courage. When my father died last year I didn't have half of your courage. You have my sympathy and my admiration.

Sincerely Yours,
Chuck Slick

> 4075 Paces Ferry Road
> Atlanta, Georgia
> November 27, 1963
>
> Dear Mrs. Kennedy,
>
> My name is Chuck Slick, and I am sure that you have never heard of me. But naturally I have heard of you and my heart goes out to you.
>
> I think that a tragedy has befallen the country and the free world. For when the United States of America loses a leader, the West and agreeing free nations of the East receive a dire setback.
>
> Having been born in Texas, I felt nauseated when I was told of this frightening blow. It makes me angry at Dallas, even though my half-brother lives there.
>
> Also I must say that I admire your courage. When my father died last year I didn't have half of your courage. You have my sympathy and my admiration.
>
> Sincerely Yours,
> Chuck Slick

🙟 *Theodore Heizer; handwritten letter*

Oconomowoc, Wisconsin
November 22, 1963

Dear Mrs. Kennedy and Children,

It is a rainy, cold, nasty night here in Oconomowoc tonight. About six o'clock I started to deliver Milwaukee Journals that contain the saddest news in my lifetime.

I am very sorry about what happened today and I hope it never happens again.

I heard about it in school today. My math teacher who is also my English teacher was too brokenhearted to teach and the students were too brokenhearted to learn. We were all listening to the radio for the latest reports concerning the assassination.

I hope the criminal is caught and when caught I hope he is punished in the best way.

Very truly sincerely yours,
Ted Heizer, age 12

Many children from Dallas wrote with painful awareness. A fourth-grade girl from Dallas sent drawings of the First Couple along with an apology: "I'm so sorry . . . I hope you don't think all people in Dallas are like that." Lindy Story, a slightly older girl from the same city, mentioned the shame of her hometown but pointed out that "every city has a maniac in it."

🖙 *Debbie Fletcher from Vienna, Virginia; handwritten letter*

Dear Mrs. Kennedy,

I am sorry to hear about Mr. Kennedy. On our current event program they think highly of P. Kennedy, I think P. Kennedy was the best P. we ever had. The physical fitness helped make me more active now I play on a soft ball team, play baseball, and football all because Mr. Kennedy started fitness. If he wasn't P. we would have made many mistakes. I admire you too because in public you are very pretty and you didn't cry (I would have). I have all my dolls named Jackie Kennedy. . . . I am 10 years old.

Yours truly,
Debbie Fletcher

P.S. I think they should have a monument and a stamp for Mr. Kennedy.

Teenagers especially often struggled to overcome their own emotions when they wrote letters. Like many her age, Linda Wells, a sixteen-year-old from Medford, Massachusetts, wrote Jacqueline Kennedy that she had found comfort in a poem that began to circulate among schools throughout the country entitled "Special Delivery from Heaven"; she enclosed it along with her own long letter. The poem's rhyming verses imagined a smiling President Kennedy consoling his wife and children as he reviewed his own funeral from paradise. Betty Lois King, from Marshall, Texas, was "sure I speak for every Negro," when she said "Cheers to the Great President." Disbelief was as common a reaction among teenagers as adults. Karen Lyn Koch of San Francisco told Mrs. Kennedy about a friend who had to have the announcement repeated five times while another "said out loud 'He can't be.'" Maureen Amira, a high school student from Long Island, wrote Mrs. Kennedy on November 22 that the day had taught her "that you don't realize how great a person is or how much he is needed, until tragedy strikes." Other teenagers used sophisticated language, such as the boy from Brooklyn who wrote to Mrs. Kennedy in an effort to "beguile" her and "assuage the anguish of your bereavement."

ʒ◆ *Penny Griffin; handwritten letter*

January 20, 1964

Dear Mrs. Kennedy,

I hardly know what to say to a person of your grandeur because I am only a thirteen year old girl, in the eighth grade. I shall always share your grief, and not because I know you, but because I love and respect you and your children.

I live in Waco, Texas but I saw you and the President at the airport on that day in Dallas. You and your husband were just as I had dreamed, so radiant, and perfect, the "symbol of America's youth." I have always wanted to meet you and maybe, when I visit Washington this summer, I will have the honor.

I realize you will remember Texas with unending sorrow and pain, and I too am ashamed but not of Texas, for I love her, but instead the tragic evils conceived in the minds of men.

In closing I would like to thank you for the many wonderful things that you did for America as her First Lady, far exceeding all others you gave to her forever your beloved husband.

Sincerely,
Penny Griffin

In one letter, an Alaskan girl took the opportunity to ask the First Lady several questions that intrigued her:

֍ *Alice J. Flynn; handwritten letter*

Tununak, Alaska
11-26-63

Dear Mrs. Kennedy

I am an Eskimo girl from Tununak, Alaska the 49th State. I am fourteen years old. My birthday is October 7, 1949. Here at Tununak there are not many people, but there are thirty-five houses in Tununak. . . . Our priest name is Rev. James E. Jacobson. He is Catholic. Not many people are Catholic you know. Do you have a plan to visit Alaska someday? I want to ask you a few questions. When you visited Turkey did they have freedom and educated? Did you visit Europe? If so would you tell us about it. These questions must be queer to you, but it isn't to me.

May god Bless You Always and make You Happy Forever

Sincerely yours
Alice J. Flynn

At least one teenager found an enduring way to commemorate her President's death:

∂ *Sandi Jones; handwritten letter*

Jones Tree Farm
Shelton, Connecticut
September 4, 1964

Dear Mrs. Kennedy,

Over on the next hill about a mile away there is a monstrous Norway Spruce planted on the day of Mr. Lincoln's death. It is the one remaining tree of twelve that a man planted there a hundred years ago.

On that black day last November I asked my father for two blue spruce to plant in memory of your wonderful husband. Dad gave them to me and I planted them and they lived through their first winter and are growing fine. They are only about a foot tall now but I certainly hope they will grow forever because your husband did not save America he saved the world from being blown to bits.

How you had and have the courage to face life and the world is beyond me. I believe you are braver than any war hero and its too bad all people couldn't have your virtues.

I know I'll never forget your courage on that day last November and of the next few days. Even 50 years from now when I'm 64 I know I'll remember as clearly as I do this minute the shock, the grief, and how I cried my eyes out, and prayed for you and he.

Very sincerely yours,
Sandi Jones

Men and women who had just reached maturity often reacted to the President's death with a new determination to carry on with his goals.

Barry Ernstoff, a student at Columbia College, in New York City, wrote that the President was "something of an idol" whose image would "always be before my eyes" in whatever profession he entered—including, possibly, politics. Twenty-one-year-old Scott B. Wells complained of no longer being able to cast his first vote in favor of President Kennedy and composed a eulogy that applauded JFK's "work, his ideals, his love and devotion" for having provided continuing direction to us and "our sons . . . the men of the future."

&🙟 *Eddie Breinan, student at Rensselaer Polytechnic; handwritten letter*

11/22/63

Dear Mrs. Kennedy—

It is a sad paradox that when one possesses the most, one also risks the most. . . . My opinion of President Kennedy was undoubtedly among the highest. Nobody can deny that he was a truly great man. . . . His assassination today was truly tragic and left me and most of my friends downright angry and ashamed. . . . It was just so wrong.

. . . Mr. Kennedy set a fine example to members of my generation. His faith in human nature and his trust and belief in his fellow man was part of what made him great. I feel that this was on the most part well-founded, but . . . it has . . . proven inadequate in one specific case. The incident has . . . caused me to resolve to work for a world in which a brave and great man may give himself to his people and not get shot in return. Had he been a cowering intellectual or an ultraconservative he might be alive at this time . . . I sincerely hope that others of my generation will . . . join me . . . to make the nation into the one that President Kennedy wanted to make it into. . . .

Eddie Breinan
Student Rensselaer Polytechnic Institute
Troy, New York

Sixteen-year-old Bill Clinton shaking hands with JFK in the Rose Garden, July 24, 1963; Clinton was in Washington as a delegate from Arkansas to the Boys Nation Convention. *Arnie Sachs/Polaris*

To some college-age students, Assistant Secretary of Labor Patrick Moynihan's off-the-cuff remark on television that "we will never be young again," seemed disturbingly real, as shown in this letter:

   F. Joseph Mackey III; typed letter to Time *magazine, forwarded to Jacqueline Kennedy*

Sir:

    Although I am only twenty-one, I can hear wide-eyed grandchildren asking me to explain the events of November 22, 1963, and I feel old. But more dramatically my youth seemed to die when the assassin's venom put an abrupt end to a certain intangible and sensitive vitality, inherent in space age enthusiasm, which was personified by John F. Kennedy in charm, health, intelligence, wit, unbounded conviction and style. Like Cinderella at one minute past midnight, should I respect my ideal images or reluctantly accept the present as my generation, my reality?

F. Joseph Mackey III
Glencoe, Illinois

Nine

A HERO TO EVERY AMERICAN

Someone who loved President Kennedy, but who had never known him, wrote to me this winter: "The hero comes when he is needed. When our belief gets pale and weak, there comes a man out of that need who is shining—and everyone living reflects a little bit of that light—and stores up some against the time when he is gone." —JACQUELINE KENNEDY, 1964

*J*ack Kennedy's hero status, earned early and offhandedly through his PT boat exploits, was amplified through his campaigns and the theme of his Pulitzer-winning book, *Profiles in Courage.* By 1960 it had become such an intrinsic component of his appeal that Norman Mailer felt it only natural to entitle his pre-election *Esquire* piece about JFK's triumph at the Democratic convention "Superman Comes to the Supermarket." Whatever bits and pieces were torn off JFK's hero image by the murky stress of day-to-day politics, the assassination immediately restored. When after a few days Jacqueline Kennedy lent official recognition to a few lines of the lead song from the musical *Camelot*—"Don't let it be forgot / That once there was a spot, / For one brief, shining moment / That was known as Camelot," the Kennedy legend was confirmed and solidified. For a while, everybody seemed to see Kennedy as a hero.

The mythic quality of the Kennedy legend helped bind the country back together, if only temporarily; it also provided a psychological bridge for those hit hard by the event. Recriminations were few; there was no social breakdown. Most significantly, a wave of sympathy for the late President's unfulfilled goals ensured passage of major civil rights legislation

Jack and Jackie Kennedy at the Inaugural Ball, Washington, D.C., January 20, 1961. *Paul Schutzer, Time & Life Pictures/Getty Images*

and the social initiatives of the "Great Society" proposed by Lyndon Johnson.

At the same time, the mythic nature of the legend ensured that over time historians and politicians would try to destroy it. A widespread reaction against Kennedy hero worship did not come, however, until the 1970s and '80s. In the first weeks after November 22 it seemed that every living American was searching to attach himself in one way or another to the great shining light that had been John Fitzgerald Kennedy. So many of the letters to Mrs. Kennedy mention the most casual connection to the President that one is tempted to think that every person who ever glimpsed John F. Kennedy at a political gathering took a stab at writing a letter to his wife. But many of these letters are also poignant, and some unusual. Sharon Ross, a Saturday helper in candidate Kennedy's 1960 Baltimore campaign office, tried to explain the incredible sense of security she had felt during his term in office, even though "during the Cuban Missile Crisis I honestly thought I was going to die." John J. MacIntyre Jr., a young man from Boston, said that to save himself from giving in to discouragement when he was downcast, he would think of the burdens on the late President.

A letter from Vesta I. Nelson, a mother in Orlando, Florida, enclosed an emotional letter from her son. He had been unable to write her for several days, he said, because "the tears would blind me." After cataloguing the many reasons he wept—for himself, for JFK and family, for "liberals and intellects . . . for politics . . . for America . . . for the world"—he hoped nonetheless that the ideals JFK stood for would continue to guide all Americans. In a brash but moving letter, Jacob Govern of Brooklyn addressed himself directly to his "noble and magnetic president" with deep sorrow, declaring that "you have not died in vain, our Prince." A letter of condolence from Florida shows how quickly the general public caught on to Jackie Kennedy's promotion of the famous verses from *Camelot* as a touchstone for remembering her husband. The article by Theodore White that quoted her had been published in *Life* magazine on December 2.

Jean (Mrs. Arthur) Yehle; handwritten letter

Key Biscayne, Florida
December 7, 1963

Dear Mrs. Kennedy,

An article by Theodore White that I read today prompted me to write to you to tell you how we, like so many others, share your loss.

The line from "Camelot" expresses our feelings perfectly. For one brief shining moment we saw Camelot. We were inspired to change our lives, to sell our business and send my husband back to the University to work toward a Ph.D., so that he might teach and do research, and we both might feel we were part of the effort the President was making to guide and shape our changing world.

We strongly feel that the man makes the times, that the hero theory of history has validity. We, like you, think there'll never be another Camelot again.

Our deepest empathy is with you.

Sincerely,
Jean Yehle

A Californian spoke for a prevalent feeling in the American public:

⁊♥ *Tom Emmitt; typewritten letter*

December 3, 1963

My dear Mrs. Kennedy:

Through the United States and all over the world, there are millions of people like me. We do not move in important social circles; we do not make decisions which influence the lives of huge numbers of our neighbors; nor do we often write letters to public figures to express our thoughts and feelings. We are seldom even visited by the pollsters who profess to know how we think.

We are, in short, the millions who have been dumbly suffering with you since the moment of the murder of your fine husband—and our good and great President. Surely nothing I can say can mitigate your grief and the sorrow of your children. . . . I can only do what I know many of the voiceless ones are doing. I can only pledge you that the influence which your husband had on us and our country—the world, in fact—will not be allowed to wither because we have forgotten. . . .

Very truly yours,
Tom Emmitt

The mother of nine children from White Bear Lake in the north country of Minnesota wrote the following letter:

November 25th, 1963

Dear Mrs. Kennedy,

. . . I am watching from my living room the greatest hero of our time, a saint and martyr, who will never, never die in our hearts. . . .

Oh, Jacqueline, how I pray. I hope you don't mind me calling you Jacqueline. You are such a brave heroine, but you feel like a friend—to everyone; not just me. You see, Jackie, I have 6 sons of my own, just growing up, and my prayers are that they can be just half as brave, just 1/10th the man that your husband was. . . .

I have three girls too, whom I shall try to pattern after you. . . .

It is difficult to say everything that is in my heart, because the children are running around me, and I forget some of the things I wanted to say. We sang "My Country Tis of Thee" after mass yesterday, and it seemed like a prayer. In fact everything seems like a prayer today. I offer all my work for you and your family today, Jacqueline. I am just ironing and cooking, and doing my work but I will try to be patient today and ask God to help me raise good children, which is my only real job. If I never knew before, I know right now what my purpose is. Your husband has not died in vain, because I know many Americans . . . are ready to rededicate their lives & ask God to help us build strong, unselfish, God-fearing, good Americans, who would proudly die for their country & their God as he did. . . .

. . . I hereby make this pledge, to do everything in my power as a mother to try to build a better America through my children. I shall never forget this day, Never! All I ask is the courage to be able to raise your kind of American instead of the kind who destroyed him. . . .

God bless you from the bottom of my heart. I am honored to have lived in your time.

Sincerely,
Mrs. Lawrence Oaks

And from the Missouri heartland came this Thanksgiving message:

Mr and Mrs. Ernst Braun; handwritten letter

November 28, 1963

Dear Mrs. Kennedy,

. . . Some force which I hardly understand compels me to write, regardless of being a citizen you don't know.

Today is Thanksgiving and would ordinarily be a happy one. Yet we can't be festive in our house. The nightmare which began last Friday afternoon is too much with us. We are grateful, though, for many things: the wonderful two years and ten months we have had while you and President Kennedy were in the White House; your vitality; your nobility; your devotion to the arts; and your affirmation of the principles of justice and human rights.

Somehow we just felt secure knowing you and President Kennedy were there. It wasn't necessary to know you personally, because we loved you with the warmth and respect that only Americans can feel for a great President and his equally great Lady. You were both right for us, and we were better people because of you.

Now that tragedy has so cruelly taken our President from us it is difficult to find our way out of the darkness of this past week. We are finding it, though, especially with your help. . . .

My husband and I extend to you and your family our deepest sympathy—a sympathy so intense we have never felt anything like it before.

> Very sincerely yours
> Mr. and Mrs. Ernst Braun

Mrs. Velma Delores Tennant from West Virginia announced to Mrs. Kennedy that having found out the day after JFK's funeral that she was going to have twins, she and her husband had decided to name them Jack

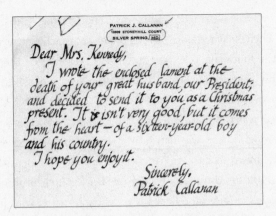

and Jackie so that they would "always be reminded of the two great people their names symbolize." Susan J. Davis of Chula Vista, California, wrote directly to John Jr. She felt certain that "You, little John" would "always wear your name with pride . . . Grow up little man, and help this country on its way."

A year after the event, emotions still remained high. Betty Jacobs, who had heard of the assassination while out shopping for "Christmas wrappings" at Filene's Warehouse in Needham, Massachusetts, wrote Mrs. Kennedy the following year that she had "never entered the store since and probably never can again without having a wave of sickness and disbelief come over me."

Perhaps it was the way John Fitzgerald Kennedy so clearly savored his own Irish roots, but newly naturalized and soon-to-be citizens seemed particularly drawn to the first American president who identified himself with an American ethnic group. Marlene Lefebvre, an immigrant living in Los Angeles, credited the First Lady and her husband with her decision in 1964 to become a citizen. Karin Rocheford, a German woman who had married an American Air Force man and moved with him to Woonsocket, Rhode Island, wrote to the First Lady in the fractured English she was valiantly attempting to learn that "Mrs. Kennebbe" was "so nice I have to name me babe for yoo."

Some recent immigrants had more direct connections with the President:

ᴓ *Peter Maroulis; handwritten letter*

New York Merchant Tailoring Co.
Washington, D.C.
12-16-63

Dear Mrs. Kennedy:

. . . When I first arrived in the United States as a poor immigrant boy from Greece I never thought that one day I would be selected to serve our President by being allowed to clean and press his clothes. . . . I, a humble immigrant from the historic but poor island of Ithaca to be given such an honor! When I wrote about it to my relatives in Greece they did not believe it. Even though Greece was the cradle of Democracy, the U.S.A. has given it a new meaning.

Again, I am sorry.

If I can be of any service to you and your family, please do not hesitate to ask me.

Sincerely,

Peter Maroulis

And at least one Russian immigrant family felt a special bond because of America's World War II alliance with the Soviet Union:

ᘓ *Dr. Mary Adelman, Julian Adelman, and family; handwritten letter*

Dear Mrs. Jacqueline Kennedy

We came from the distant Russian city—Gorki on the River Volga. We left 2 year ago our homeland Russia, our beautiful Russian language, very many friends—I my M.D. career, my husband his teacher job, because we could not stand more Krushchow Propaganda about American animosity to the Russian people. . . . During World War II, I and my husband did our best in our Soviet Units to resist the villainous German Nationalism. . . . I was then only 22 year old.

I finished my medical-school and first training and immediately was mobilized to help our young Russian soldiers. . . . Under heavy artillery shells we did our job in surgery and very often with bare hands. . . . We were exhausted and in this time you Americans came with your moral help, food, medicine, even US made bullets and artillery shells. . . . Twice America fought with Russia against Germany and we fight now each other: could be the biggest crime! . . .

I hoped that from the free America will come the salvation. Our late President—your husband and father began this job . . . I was sure he will be reelected. . . .

Dear Jacqueline—this sad for all of us day came very soon. I remember I could not help to cry the whole Friday. I felt like somebody had hit me over my head and took a part of my soul—my hope. Very many bad thoughts tortured me and my family. Why is allowed to carry guns? Why is permitted to sell weapons to ex-convicts? Where in the civilized World will you find such "freedom" to kill. It seems to me thousands of men are dying on the streets in U.S.A., victims of the criminals. In Dallas you are reading every day about killings. Add to this stealings, robberies, rapes and racial violence and you are giving the best propaganda for Krushchow.

Mrs. Kennedy! There are many possibilities to finish this infamy. Don't go away from politics. You have to go on with the ideas of your late husband. Only in this affairs you will find healing and keep away dreary thoughts. Begin, please, and you will gain the crown of your late husband.

Yours sincerely, Dr. Mary Adelman, Julian Adelman and family

One anonymous sympathizer arranged to have Mrs. Kennedy sent a single white rose every Friday for four weeks from Washington's Nosegay Flower Shop, accompanied by inspirational verses from Psalm 139, *Siddhartha,* and the Upanishads. More commonly expressed, however, was faith in the traditional Christian God and an afterlife. Indeed, "the will of God" was invoked more regularly in the letters sent Mrs. Kennedy than any other phrase. An example of this kind of letter came from Chicago:

?❧ *Mrs. Leo Domzalski; handwritten letter*

December 4, 1963

Dear Mrs. Kennedy:

I've never written to the White House before but I felt like I just had to write. . . .

When I first heard the news about the President I kept wondering why it all had to happen especially now when we needed him so. . . . The only reason I could think of was because it was the will of God. Why He did it now surely is hard to understand but I think it's the only good reason.

I shall always remember the President, also you and the children, in my prayers and Holy Communion when I go to mass.

Sincerely,

Mrs. Leo Domzalski

Mass cards—remembrance cards that promised a certain number of Masses to be said in the name of the departed—also made up a substantial portion of all the mail that arrived on Mrs. Kennedy's doorstep after November 22. Some of the religiously inclined went further than simply sending a Mass card. Carmen Fitzgerald of Aguadilla, Puerto Rico, who referred in her message of November 24 to several other letters sent previously, said she had "dreamed that he died in office" and recalled the advice she had given in earlier messages to Jackie to seek counsel in "the Scriptures and memorize Psalm 22. Be of good courage, look up, Jesus loves you." Susanna Faslett, a fourth-grade girl from the Holy Spirit School, invited Mrs. Kennedy to come see her parish window, where a picture of the President had replaced the stained-glass window of St. John the Baptist. A woman from Harrisburg, Pennsylvania, wrote Jacqueline Kennedy about a dream she had the day before the assassination in which she saw the President in "a beautiful bright blue sky . . . lying dead" with the kneeling Virgin Mary cradling "his head on her lap" and weeping tears over his "beloved . . . face."

In his eulogy for the fallen President, the Roman Catholic televangelist Bishop Fulton Sheen stated, "On a brighter Easter Day we will see that our national brotherhood was purchased by the blood of a victim, John Fitzgerald Kennedy." The association of religious and political symbolism also featured in this letter from the Mother Superior of Ursuline Academy in Great Falls, Montana:

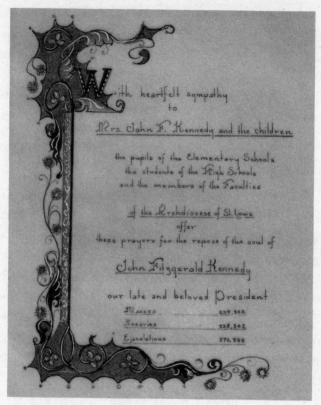

With heartfelt sympathy
to

Mrs. John F. Kennedy and the children

the pupils of the Elementary Schools
the students of the High Schools
and the members of the Faculties

of the Archdiocese of St. Louis
offer
these prayers for the repose of the soul of

John Fitzgerald Kennedy

our late and beloved President

Masses	228,342
Rosaries	228,542
Ejaculations	570,865

Mass card from the Archdiocese of St. Louis.

Mother M. Monica Reardon; typewritten letter

Nov. 30, 1963

My dear Mrs. Kennedy and Children:

. . . Here in Great Falls . . . where many of us, Sisters as well as hundreds of others, shook hands with him, his passing meant . . . the loss of one near and dear to us.

One of our Sisters here made a touching comparison of his death with that of Our Lord's: like our Lord, she said, he was put to death on Friday between the hours of twelve and three after a short period of about three years of service, love, and devotion for all mankind, even for those bent on destroying him. And I had to add, dear Jacqueline, how like our Blessed Mother, who stood at the Foot of the Cross of her slain Christ, you were as you held your beloved slain one in your arms and stood strong and heroic through all your sorrow. . . .

Sincerely in Our Lord,
Mother M. Monica Reardon, O.S.U.

The many messages from members of minority groups testify to President Kennedy's strong magnetism for the marginalized and disadvantaged. In a half-page typewritten note to the First Lady, Ernan H. Smith—an engineer in the power plant of Latter Day Saints Hospital in Salt Lake City, who described himself as a "nobody from nowhere" whose heart bled "for you and the nation"—reminisced about seeing the President in Utah in September. From the White Buffalo Council, an alliance of tribal nations publishing a bulletin entitled *The Indian Times,* arrived a "tribute to your Chief, and ours." Walter W. McDonald, a Native American member of the Confederated Salish-Kootenai Tribes and President of the Montana Inter-Tribal Policy Board, deplored the "hate and confusion" responsible for the tragedy and called for the "American people" to "come closer together." A first-generation Mexican-American, mailman Henry Gonzales of El Paso, identified himself as "but a humble postman" in his typewritten letter to Mrs. Kennedy. He wanted the First Lady to know that "we Texans of Mexican descent had a great love for all of you" and to not think that "all of us Texans were bad."

Many prisoners and former prisoners wrote to Mrs. Kennedy. Inmate No. 80398 from the prison in Leavenworth, Kansas, sent a letter to President Johnson asking him to "convey to Mrs. Kennedy that not only the Rich, the Poor, the Good the Bad, but also we who have been the ones to owe a debt to society . . . also wish to express our deep sorrow to her and family for the loss of our President, who we so dearly loved and respected." Some offered a kind of self-sacrifice. Maude Oberg, an elderly woman living in a "Ministering Friends" Home for needy women in Miami, wondered "why an old woman like me could not have died in his place." And Prisoner No. 107635, serving time in a workhouse prison in Occoquan, Virginia, wrote Mrs. Kennedy, "Were it in my power that I could have given my life in exchange for his, I would've been highly honored to have done so."

Those who mourned the President included political adversaries. Susan Sandberg, a self-described "bitter opponent" of the President's from Libertyville, Illinois, wrote: "I cannot now find anywhere in my being one shred of gladness that this event took place." Nancy Fash from Darien, Connecticut, wrote for herself and her husband as two Republicans who sent their love and respect. A public relations executive from New York City who had met Jack Kennedy as a little boy on Boston's South Shore and could not imagine "that little boy as President," now found "not a little boy but a symbol of all that each should cherish in this world" and regretted having never supported him politically. Major General Julius Klein (Ret.), a self-described "Taft Republican," wrote from Chicago that he regretted not being able to boast that he had voted for JFK. And he reported that, while watching the marathon television coverage, his grandniece had asked, "Is the President now with George Washington?"

Not all letters that arrived in Washington were heedful of the woman they wrote to, and some seemed to tie their messages of sympathy to personal interest. The mother of a country music singer from Texas wrote asking the First Lady to help her arrange for the recording of a song her son had written about the assassination called "The Last Hour." And one man from a Baltimore suburb registered a respectful request that Mrs. Kennedy reconsider the "acreage allotment" in Arlington Cemetery because such a large plot "shades his memory and removes him from us." During the summer of 1964 a rumor circulated that Mrs. Kennedy was rewarding handsomely those who sent her dollar bills bearing the *K* mark (for Dallas Federal Reserve). One "donor" of two such bills was careful to ask for the return of his paper money if his information was wrong— a request social secretary Nancy Tuckerman was more than happy to fulfill.

Some Americans took an aphoristic approach in their letters of sympathy. Myro J. Dent, a San Diego man, wrote *Time* magazine that a janitor he met had talked about the death of the President as an open book: "The pictures are there, but I can't read the words."

ॐ *Donald J. Ciappenelli; letter to* Time *magazine*

December 6, 1963

Sir:

It will take another hundred years to create another man equal to the one cut down in one second by an assassin's bullet.

Donald J. Ciappenelli
University of Massachusetts
Amherst, Mass.

ॐ *Joyce Bishop; handwritten note*

Nov. 22, 1963

Dear Mrs. Kennedy,

Thank God life is not measured by a cradle and a grave.

In Christ,
Joyce Bishop

Some writers were prompted to philosophical disquisitions to their closest friends or family. The sister of one such writer was so affected by what she received that she forwarded it to Mrs. Kennedy, believing it "should be put in the Kennedy Library."

≈ *Richard V. Santoro; typewritten letter to his sister Barbara Santoro Longsworth, forwarded to Mrs. Kennedy*

November 22, 1963

Dear Barbara,

Of all human conditions surely reality is the most difficult to grasp. The statement—The President has been shot—is insane. It simply cannot come to pass that here . . . in these civilized lands, a leader would be cut down by some obscure rancorous assassin. But it did happen—and we must, beyond an irrational sense of personal loss, evaluate the enormous implications of this act of violence. Kennedy . . . may well have been the last of a line of individuals, spawned and educated in New England, who viewed life as an incessant barrage of vicissitudes over which the prime virtues of honesty and idealism alone could prevail. . . . The President . . . dies unfulfilled—he challenged the people of the nation to test their preconceptions, to study the emerging world about them, to sacrifice their comforts—and his reward was more often than not an almost maddening indifference. Why should we give the niggers all those rights—why, that's discrimination in reverse! Who needs medical care plans? I'm sick and tired of handing over tax money to all those foreign countries, and besides, they're all pinko anyway!

Go tell it to a Negro, who must bear the suffocating outrage of watching his woman bring home the bread. . . .

Go tell it to that old man who broke his back all his life laying bricks and now has nothing for the doctor's bills but calluses and death. . . .

Go tell it to the thousands of people in Latin America who, a short time before the Allianza para el Progresso, found the only thing existing between their souls and utter deprivation to be their own skin. . . .

. . . Two American Presidents—Lincoln and Kennedy—attempted to translate the idealism of the Constitution into reality. The first failed, and paid with his life. The second failed, and paid with his life. . . .

Maudlin displays of grief, some sincere, others self-seeking, will deluge the press and all communications channels. Why are they so damned sorry now? . . . But, in fact, I feel that Kennedy does, or did, however incoherent the voice within us, remind us gently that we exist not for nation, or ambition, or power, or money or comfort, but primarily for the good we can do each other. . . .

His death is disquieting to me beyond reason, perhaps, but the death of an ideal is profoundly worse. It is that his great talents were not enough for the task—what now will lesser men do? . . .

Love,
Dick

Robert Kirkpatrick from San Francisco sent as his condolence to Jacqueline Kennedy a list of the great men JFK could be compared with: Socrates, Jesus, Lincoln, and Gandhi, among others. "He stands exalted," wired Milwaukee residents Mr. and Mrs. Alton Shimek. A woman from New Jersey reported to Mrs. Kennedy that she had sent a letter to Richard Cardinal Cushing requesting that he start the procedures required to have John Fitzgerald Kennedy officially declared a Catholic Saint.

Still, Americans looked to the future. And the future that most interested them, more even than the political future of the *other* Kennedy brothers, was the future of Jackie, the hero's companion. When Mrs. Jean Winchester of Lexington, elected "Mrs. Massachusetts" for 1963, complimented the First Lady for her "courageous composure" that had "been an inspiration to women all over the world," she was merely echoing a message that ran through nearly every one of the hundreds of thousands of items of mail that descended on the White House. Many of those messages had concrete advice and suggestions for the now former First Lady; some simply pleaded for her not to go away. Among the requests: "please do not withdraw from us"; "stay in Washington"; "continue in some form of public life"; "continue your work as a cultural leader"; "continue your interests in [the White House] furnishings"; "narrate or write [a book about JFK] as husband and father" or about "JFK the boy," or write any book; "found a religious Order." An approximate list of the other roles and/or positions correspondents expected her to play in the future of the country: minister plenipotentiary; Ambassador to Latin America or France (a frequent suggestion); roving international ambassador at large; Secretary of Health, Education, and Welfare; administrator of the Medicare program if and when it was enacted into law; a new UN position with the title "First Lady of the World for Peace"; head of American Pioneer Trails Association; the new post of "Secretary of Culture" (many such requests); a new position as "White House Historian"; a position in the cabinet; U.S. Senator, then President; President (many times); Vice President (the most frequent request).

One correspondent seemed to see through to the very essence of Jacqueline Kennedy:

ॐ *Sister M. E. Michael; typewritten letter*

> Union Catholic High School
> Girls' Department
> Scotch Plains, New Jersey
> December 1, 1963

My dear Mrs. Kennedy,

"There are places in our souls which do not exist until Suffering enters in and brings them into existence." Three years ago as I studied your face during the inauguration ceremonies, I saw the door to one of those deep places open, and I prayed: "God, be kind. Be kind to her; she was born to suffer." And when his beautiful challenge shattered the winter sunlight, I prayed for you again, thinking: "He is asking you to give more than any of us. He asks you to give your husband."

And now we have given him back. That is the only beautiful thing in this horrible hour: he is yours again irrevocably. Through all those public ceremonies you were giving him to us and us to him, but for all that he is yours again. . . . No one can ever take him from you again. . . .

Léon Bloy has written of the Virgin Mary, "She . . . is the Queen of Angels, and she weeps. Angels cannot cry, but she can. And that is why she is their Queen." I thought of this when I watched you standing through those three eulogies. I detest nuns who make Biblical comparisons lightly, but I could not resist. You were the image of the Mother of God. You, too, *stood* for your crucifixion.

I have said that I began praying for you three years ago, but during those four days and nights, I prayed for you without ceasing. I felt that if I stopped for a moment, even to sleep, that you would fall apart. But you didn't fall apart, you held thirty million people together. When I returned to school Tuesday, I still couldn't bear to leave you. So I didn't. In literature classes I taught, "Forget whatever poems I have read to you. Read Jacqueline Kennedy. She *is* poetry." In French class I taught, "Forget what I have tried to tell you of the spirit, the grace, the passion of the real French aristocrat. Remember forever that you have seen the spirit, the grace, the passion of Jacqueline Bouvier." As a teacher of adolescent girls I could say at last, "You have heard me say that the difference between a girl and a woman was pain, and you have thought this a grim warning. But now that you have witnessed her exquisite agony, you know that this is a glorious promise."

Sincerely,

Sister M. E. Michael, O.P.

P.S. None of the above is the sentimental effusion of a "fan." I never voted for your husband.

The thousands of condolence letters written to Jacqueline Kennedy offer the snapshot of a world in shock and a nation in mourning. President Kennedy had summoned Americans to a "new frontier" that promised an unprecedented projection of United States international influence abroad as well as social justice at home. The vision not only made sense to many in the generation that had emerged with unbridled optimism from World War II, but held great appeal for its children, the baby boom that came to maturity in the 1960s.

With Kennedy gone, his successor not only claimed his mantle, but professed to go him one better. *Camelot* might be giving way to *Hello, Dolly!* but also it did not matter: dreamers and idealists still found hope in LBJ's promise to limit armed conflict abroad and build a Great Society at home. As Jackie's silent stoicism proved enduring and she withdrew from the public scene, the allegiance of many liberals shifted to Bobby Kennedy, who eventually began to voice the discomfort many felt but repressed in the days immediately after November 22. Full disillusionment, full-scale war in Vietnam, and the radical alienation of the younger generation was yet to come. For now, the shots of November were aberrations, not omens. The New Frontier still beckoned—and there was nothing to do but march on bravely wherever it led.

NOTE ON THE LETTERS

$\mathcal{S}$pelling and grammar of individual documents, and to a lesser degree punctuation, have been retained in the texts included here, except where failing to correct them might prove misleading or a distraction to the larger sense of the original. Some formal consistency has been introduced for the letters (placement of date and address, salutation, etc.), while the telegrams are presented so as to resemble the originals as much as possible. The original language of letters and telegrams not written in English has been noted.

ACKNOWLEDGMENTS

To say that this book owes as much to the writers of the letters collected here as to the two authors on its title page is self-evident. But my personal debt to the condolence correspondents of a half century ago goes deeper and feels more intimate than that of collector and editor. Reading their words of sympathy, listening to their voices emerge from the pages during hours of reading, sorting, and sifting, I came to see how my own sad memory of walking home from junior high school that November day was inextricably linked with the reactions of millions of others around the globe. Unlike me, these men, women, and children had recorded their reactions and emotions and sent them off to be shared with the president's widow. My own memory was layered with the patina of nostalgia, but the letters I read were raw with pain yet energized by hope. Bound together by a common grief and ideals inspired by both Jack and Jacqueline Kennedy, they offered a picture of common humanity refracted in endlessly different ways by a single event in time. So let me express my gratitude first of all to all those who wrote to Jacqueline Kennedy. To you whom I came to know slightly in the process of securing permissions, either directly or from your heirs; to you whom I never located; to you from whom I secured permission whose letters ultimately could not be included for reasons of space; to you whose letters I barely skimmed or rushed over altogether: thanks to all.

That these letters still exist for us to marvel at is a testament first of all to the vision and enterprise of Jacqueline Kennedy and the special devotion and organizational skills of Nancy Tuckerman and Pamela Turnure. It is also a tribute to the dedication of the thousands of volunteers who were the first readers of over a million pieces of correspondence, and the commitment on the part of the archival staff at the Kennedy Library. Let me offer a brief summary of the collection's history. Once the volunteers' first sorting was accomplished, the condolence collection came under the auspices of the John F. Kennedy Library. The perseverance of most of its librarians, curators, and archivists has succeeded in preserving and maintaining a significant portion of this huge collection of condolence mail, even though it does not fit naturally with many of the other papers. Parts of the collection, however, suffered warehouse water damage during the fifteen-year interregnum between the founding of the library and the opening of the library building. The processing and cataloguing of the condolence mail was finally begun in 1983, twenty years after President Kennedy's death. Around this time a controversial decision was made, strongly disapproved by the current archival staff, to cull all the undamaged condolence correspondence by "scientific" sampling. As a result of the water damage and culling, the number of items in the condolence collection has dropped from some one and a quarter million items to about 204,000.

For decades the condolence collection at the JFK Library was largely forgotten by researchers. In the fall of 2007 the original author of this volume, Jay Mulvaney, who had already written sevc.al books about the Kennedys, turned his attention to the subject and easily convinced St. Martin's Press of its appeal. Tragically, he died of a heart attack a few months after beginning this project, completing an initial selection of several thousand letters, and securing several dozen permissions from important correspondents. In

September 2008 I inherited his excellent proposal, outline, and collection of material. Thank you, Jay—you were the one who first thought of making a book from the condolence collection, and the idea will forever remain yours to claim. I only wish I could have met you in person; fond memories of you and your ebullient personality have smoothed the way for me throughout the process of researching, writing, and permission-gathering. Many thanks also to your beloved sister Paula Cashin, whose goodwill and assistance here been instrumental in assuring that your vision of this book would be realized.

Jay was a regular at the JFK Library in Boston, which under the supervision of the recently-retired chief archivist Allan Goodrich, was assiduous in its care and management of the condolence (and all other) collections. I would particularly like to thank Steven Plotkin and Sharon Kelly for their assistance during my many days at the library, along with Michael Desmond and the interns and other staff. In the audiovisual archives Maryrose Grossman, Laurie Austin, and James Hill all rendered expert advice and guidance. For providing me the warmth of family and friendship during research trips to Boston, I will always be indebted to Dennis and Nan Roth and family, as well as to Mary Jo Hughes.

I could never have conducted the research needed to provide context and historical setting for these letters without the resources provided me by the New York Public, Vassar College, and Hotchkiss School libraries, nor the assistance and dedication of the staff at my own local Cornwall Library, who have always been willing to go that extra step to procure an obscure book on interlibrary loan. Nancy Tuckerman has been of inestimable assistance in drawing for me a lively portrait of the condolence acknowledgment process and kindly reviewing my depiction of it in manuscript stage.

Collecting permissions means turning into a private detective. Luckily the wonders of search engines and the Internet have greatly accelerated the process of finding people, although I would never have found as many as I did without the assistance of more clever searchers than I: Lynn Behrendt, Rachel Bennek, and my wife Elisabeth Kaestner were the key figures here.

Along the way I found a host of other guides as well. Among them were: Betsy Aaron and Dick Threllkeld, James Abbott, Martha Maroulis Alafoginis, Marielba Alvarez at the Embassy of the Bolivarian Republic of Venezuela in the USA, Iyabe Benslimane at the Banque Internationale Arabe de Tunisie, Allyson Bethune at PT Boats Inc., the Birmingham Civil Rights Institute, Bim Bisell, Bernard Bockelmann, Elke Bockelmann, Rupert Burgess, Faye Burnell, Choate Rosemary Hall School (Judy Donald in archives, Christine Bennett in Alumni Relations), Robert Christison, Janet Couch, Patrick Cox, John Cramer, Peter Cramer, Toni Cross, Elisha D'Arcy at the High Court of Ireland, Miltiades Dartoozos, Hope Dellon, Mrs. Alex Dickie, Peter Edwards, Jacek Galazka, Dr. Vittoria Gassman, Gerald and Elly Gotzen, Louisa Hargrave, Teresa Hogue, Michael Howard, Debbie Hutnyak at Oberlin College, Aideen Ireland at the National Archives of Ireland, Sister Jacinta at the Vatican Library, Veronica L. James, Mr. Shafqat Jilil of the Pakistan Mission to the United Nations, Claudia Johnson-Nichols at the Sergeant York Patriotic Foundation, Donna B. Johnson, Marie Johnson, Mary Krienke at Sterling Lord Literistic, Mériem Bourguiba Laouiti, Laura Tyson Li, Patricia Macnaughton at Macnaughton Lord Representation, Kerry McCarthy, Sarah McNair at Alan Brodie Representation Ltd., Lars Madsen at Harvard University, Lawrence Malkin, Sister Margherita Marchione, Dr. Fray Marshall, Quinn Marshall at New Directions Publishing, John Miller, Nguyen Ngoc Bich and the National Congress of Vietnamese Americans, Helen O'Riordan at Conabury House, Augusta Pacelli, Zung Pham, Lily Phillips at the Zanuck Company, Michael Piekarski at Vassar Alumnae Relations, Jan Pottker, Marie Prentice, Sandy Quinn at the Richard Nixon Foundation, Susan Reed, Jill Roggeveen at St. Xavier University in Chicago, Nancy Smith at the Joseph P. Kennedy Jr. Foundation, Ann Miller Sperry, John Joe Spring at All Hallow's College, John Stravinsky, Aliki Strongylos, Erin Taylor at the British Embassy in Washington, D.C., Craig Tenney at Harold Ober Associates, Charles Alan Tippit, Betty Tulliy at the Mwalimu Nyerere Foundation, Luis Vassy at the French Embassy in Washington, D.C., Susan Walker at Miss Porter's School, Thomas Wauthier at Mémorial Charles de Gaulle, Robert Whitlock, Antje Winter of Adenauer Haus, Gordon Wise at Curtis Brown Ltd., Mary Alice Yates at the Guggenheim Foundation, Thomas Mark Yehle, the York (Pennsylvania) Historical Society, Stephen Wadsworth Zinsser, and Anne Zinsser. Apologies in advance to those of you whom I have inadvertently left out. I also regret that we are unable to list many of those who helped Jay find the authors of letters for which he secured permissions.

While translations from the German and French in this volume are my own, I'd like to thank Jacek Galazka for translating Bolek Rey's letter from Polish, Oliviya Chavka for translating Nikita Khrushchev's telegram from Russian, and Adeline De Angelis for translating Rómulo Betancourt's telegram from Spanish.

I will always remain grateful to my agent, Madeleine Morel of 2M Communications Ltd., for thinking of me after she heard about Jay's unfortunate death. Her collaborative relationship with Jay's agent, John Silbersack of Trident Media Group, is remarkable; together they have provided smooth, consistent, and reliable service of the kind authors and editors rarely enjoy. And what a pleasure it has been to have for a publisher St. Martin's Press—the house where I once worked—and to find there not only my old friend, President and Publisher Sally Richardson, but new friends on the editorial side in the persons of Charlie Spicer and Yaniv Soha. Colleagues in the publishing business had told me in advance how "good" Charlie was with authors—and no one needs that more than an editor-turned-author. Yaniv, meanwhile, has offered incisive editorial suggestions and coolheaded practical guidance. They are a great team. Also of tremendous assistance at Macmillan/St. Martin's in dealing with permissions questions has been Diana Frost of the legal department.

Finally, to the women in my life, my wife, Elisabeth, and daughter, Addie: not only does your love hold and maintain me, but your intelligence, wit, compassion, and insight help me see better the flaws in my own work. To close, I'd like to state that despite the valuable input from experts, friends, and associates, I remain solely responsible for any errors of fact or misrepresentation in this book.

—Paul De Angelis

A MESSAGE OF THANKS
FROM PAULA CASHIN,
SISTER OF JAY MULVANEY

*F*irst I would like to acknowledge and thank all the wonderfully kind and generous individuals who saw this book through its completion, most especially John Silbersack, Charlie Spicer, and Paul De Angelis, as well as St. Martin's Press. Words cannot express my family's most sincere gratitude for having our brother's last work published. It simply would not have happened without your dedication and hard work.

Also, I would like to thank the many people who were such dear friends to Jay. During numerous conversations with him, it was obvious how much all of you meant to him, the impact you had on his life and how much he loved you all. I would specifically like to thank those of you whom Jay held very close to his heart: Signora Wanda Ferragamo, who made his time in Florence a prelude to Heaven; Lilly Pulitzer, who opened both her home and her heart to Jay; Nick Wollner, a trusted friend; all his friends and colleagues at Rockwell International; Julie Seymour, a treasure to both Jay and me; Diane McClure, whose home will always hold a part of Jay's spirit; Vasken Matteosian, there are no words for all that you meant to Jay and still mean to us; and finally, Caroline Gervase, his one true soul mate.

Most important, I would like to thank Jay himself. There are few gifts in this life that truly improve and bring more happiness with age. My brother was that one true gift to us, his family. During his life, he gave us his humor, his wisdom, his strength, and his never-ending support. In his death, he left us with a legacy of unconditional love.

So, dearest brother, on behalf of your sister Katy Mulvaney, and your much beloved nieces and nephew, Meghan, Colleen, and Kevin Cashin, find peace in your rest knowing you gave us everything we could possibly need with your love to continue on until we meet again.

Your most loving and thankful sister,
Paula Cashin

When he shall die,
Take him and cut him out in little stars,
And he will make the face of heaven so fine
That the world will be in love with night,
And pay no worship to the garish sun.
                    —*William Shakespeare*

CREDITS AND PERMISSIONS

With deep appreciation to the following parties for allowing us to reproduce the text and/or facsimiles of letters to which they hold copyright: David C. Acheson; Maria M. Adelman; Konrad Adenauer (grandson); All Hallows College and the Order of Vincentians in Ireland; the Estate of June Allyson; Marian Anderson Historical Society, Inc.; Joanne W. Armstrong; Michael Ramon Langhorne Astor; Viscount Astor; Lauren Bacall Robards; Jean-Claude Baker; the George Balanchine Trust; Shawnee Cramer Baldwin; Patricia Barry; Bouvier Beale Jr.; the Literary Executors of the late Sir Cecil Beaton; Francine Bellson; the Estate of His late Highness Maharana Bhagwat Singh Mewar; Claire Nice Bingham; Joyce Bishop; Kelly Bishop; Thomas Bockelmann; Lindy Boggs; Neïla Bourguiba; Sampson P. Bowers; Margaret D. Braun; Deborah Rachel Breinan and Howard Alan Breinan; *The Assassination of John Kennedy* by Gwendolyn Brooks, reprinted by consent of Brooks Permissions; Josiah Bunting III; Libby Byers; Francesca Calderone-Steichen; Patrick J. Callanan; Lani Campbell; Cass Canfield Jr.; Oleg Cassini; Barbara M. Casteen; the Estate of Phyllis Cerf Wagner, and to Christopher and Jonathan Cerf; Choate Rosemary Hall Archives; Donald J. Ciappenelli; Conabury House, Loreto Sisters; H. M. King Constantine; Joan Costello; NC Aventales AG, successor in title to the Estate of Noël Coward; Allison Stacey Cowles; Barbara Cramer; Alice Gloria Crayton; H. Crosby; Ciaran Cuffe; Curtis Brown Ltd., London, on behalf of the Estate of Winston Churchill; Clifton Truman Daniel; Admiral Philippe de Gaulle; Stéphane de Laage; Seble Desta; Mary F. Devenny; Angie Dickinson; Mrs. Leo Domzalski; Ilse Dorati; A. Sholto

Douglas-Home; Her Majesty's Government of the United Kingdom of Great Britain and Northern Ireland for Elizabeth and Sir Alec Douglas-Home; Hugh Downs; Penny (Griffin) Dyer; Charles P. Edwards; Her Majesty Queen Elizabeth II, © Crown copyright 2008; Queen Elizabeth the Queen Mother, the Royal Archives © 2008, HM Queen Elizabeth II; Barbara Emmitt; Christiane Engel; Katherine Winton Evans; Mrs. Myrlie Evers-Williams; Katherine F. Fay; Paul B. Fay III; Brett Ferneau; the Marshall Field family; the Firestone family; Joan Fontaine; Roberta Fulbright Foote; Mrs. Peter Forrestal; Ministry of Foreign Affairs of France; Jane Freeman; John Clark Gable; Mary Barelli Gallagher; Matthew S. Gamser; Frances T. Gates; Sherry P. Geyelin; Graham Gilmer Jr.; Billy Graham Evangelistic Association; Michael H——; Marni R. (Politte) Harmony; Helen F. Harris; Office of the President, Harvard University; Marian S. Heiskell; Brenda Heizer; Elizabeth W. Holden; Amory Houghton Jr.; Harold Ober Associates for Langston Hughes; James D. Hurd; National Archives of Ireland; Mr. Winfred James Sr.; Debbie Fletcher Johnson; Sandra Lee Jones; Patricia Ward Kelly; Brigid Kennedy; Sergei N. Khrushchev; telegram from Reverend and Mrs. Martin Luther King Sr. and Dr. and Mrs. Martin Luther King Jr. reprinted by arrangement with The Heirs to the Estate of Martin Luther King Jr., c/o Writers House as agent for the proprietor, New York, NY, Copyright 1963 Dr. Martin Luther King Jr., copyright renewed 1991 Coretta Scott King; Maurice L. Kowal; the Vivien Leigh Estate; Alexandra Leigh-Hunt; Liberace Foundation for the Performing and Creative Arts (Liberace is a registered trademark of the Liberace Foundation; the content of this telegram is the property of, and used with permission granted by, the Liberace Foundation, 1775 E. Tropicana, Las Vegas NV 89119, www.liberace .org); William F. Liebenow; the Lieberson family; Stephen Lipmann; Linda Long; the children of Sylvia Taft Lotspeich: Sylvia, Charles, and Stephen; Grand Duchy of Luxembourg; F. Joseph Mackey III; Harold Macmillan Book Trust; the Stanley Marcus family and the Stanley Marcus Trust, for permitting the use and inclusion of the Stanley Marcus letter within this book; Kathleen "Kerry" McCarthy; R. Craig McNamara; Cercle d'Etudes Jacques and Raïssa Maritain, Kolbsheim, France; the family of Dr. Victor F. Marshall; Alice J. Metz; Sister Elizabeth Michael, O.P.; HSH Prince of Monaco's Artistic Commission; Marianne Monnet; Katharine B. Morgan; Mary Morgan; Stanley G. Mortimer III; New Directions Publishing Corporation; the Niarchos family; James G. Niven; the Richard Nixon Foundation; the Mwalimu Nyerere Foundation; the Estate of Sean O'Casey; Rosemary O'Donohue; Rosella A. Oaks; Donatella Ortona; Francesco Pacelli; Farah Pahlavi; Permanent Mission of Pakistan to the United Nations; Dr. Ernst-Josef Pauw; the family of Peter James Maroulis; Nga Thi Pham (Mrs. Rau Khac

Pham); Kate Pond; Carlos Prio-Touzet; James A. Reed family; Boleslaw Rey; the Earl of Rosslyn; A. Russell-Roberts; excerpt from "When Death Came April Twelve, 1945" in *The Complete Poems of Carl Sandburg,* Revised and Expanded Edition, copyright © 1970, 1969 by Lilian Steichen Sandburg, Trustee, reprinted by permission of Houghton Mifflin Harcourt Publishing Company; Richard Santoro; Charles U. Slick; Berenice R. Spalding; Daniel E. Spitsnogle; Katherine and Spiro Stamos; Frances Sternhagen; Sheila C. (Meader) Stratton; the Stravinsky Estate; Adele Hall Sweet and Sarah Ann Kramarksy; James W. Symington; Richard Thau; Helen Thomas; Marie Tippit; Lady Anne Tree and Lady Elizabeth Cavendish; Ursuline Sisters, Great Falls, Montana; Charles Van Doren; Marianne Whitlock; Kate R. Whitney; Jean H. Winchester; Estate of Shelley Winters; David Wise; Harris Wofford; Ann Yarborough, daughter-in-law, for the Ralph Yarborough heirs; Jean T. Yehle; Sergeant York Patriotic Foundation; Richard D. Zanuck; Anne Johnson Zobec.

Grateful acknowledgment is also made here for permission from Ron Sachs and Polaris to reproduce Arnie Sachs's photograph of Bill Clinton shaking hands with John F. Kennedy; and to Getty Images for permission to reproduce Paul Schutzer's photograph of Jack and Jackie Kennedy at the Inaugural Ball; and, once again, to the dedicated Maryrose Grossman and the audiovisual department at the John F. Kennedy Library for their help in locating and selecting the other photographic images that appear in this volume.